East Cowes Castle

ISBN   1 899139 00 1

British Library Cataloguing in Publication Data.
A catalogue record for this book is available from the British Library

Published by
Business by Design
High Beeches, Camberley

Printed by
The Cannon Press
Stuart House, Plantation Row, Camberley

The typeface used for the text in this book is
New Times Roman 10 on 12pt

East Cowes Castle

THE SEAT OF

JOHN NASH Esq

A PICTORIAL HISTORY

IAN SHERFIELD

A Vision of One,
Crafted by many,
is Swept Away,
On the Winds of a
Changing World.

JOHN NASH

1752 - 1835
ARCHITECT
SEIGNEUR OF EAST COWES CASTLE

CONTENTS

Acknowledgements   7

List of Illustrations   9

Bibliographical Abbreviations   12

Introduction   13

1.   1793 - 1835: The Nash Epoch

     i)   *Associations*   14
     ii)   *Building the Castle*   20
     iii)   *The Palace*   31
     iv)   *Island Retreat*   38

2.   1835 - 1935: Post Nash, Shannon to Gort   49

3.   1935 - 1963; Decline   53

4.   The Castle -House Cycle   55

5.   The Isle of Wight Architect   63

Appendix I   John Nash, Architect 1752 - 1835 Biographical Reference   74

Appendix II   i)   Works Completed by Nash   76
     ii)   Works Attributed to Nash   82

Appendix III   East Cowes Castle and Estate Interesting Statistics   83

Appendix IV   Glossary of Terms Used in the Text   84

Appendix V   Further Reading   86

Index   87

ACKNOWLEDGEMENTS

ssentially this work is an amalgam of the efforts of many. Although my name appears on the cover, my deep appreciation must be recorded of the many that have been instrumental in its production.

Having grown up in East Cowes, virtually within the shadow of the Castle, it is perhaps not surprising, that I should want to present something of what, was a complete fascination to me. Much of the material included ,is therefore, from my personal collection of Nash memorabilia and from the recollection of those who knew the building. To whom no doubt, a revisit will be of interest, to others perhaps, surprise at the extirpation of this once noble mansion.

The late Sir John Summerson is responsible more than anyone for presenting the true picture of John Nash and through his erudite work published in 1935 and 1980, has provided a major source of information to me. Complementary to this source is the work of the late Terrence Davis, published in 1960 and 1966 and the complete catalogue of the work of John Nash compiled by the late Michael Mansbridge and published in 1991. I must also thank Patricia Drummond, research secretary to the late Sir John Summerson for her encouragement throughout.

There have been a number of other sources of information that I have accessed to supplement my own, these considerably reinforcing the presentation with some previously unpublished material. First and foremost I must thank Mr Peter Laing, a descendant of Sir James Pennethorne, whose help and hospitality has been inspirational. Peter, a very busy person, gave generously of his time, access to the Nash papers and has allowed me to reproduce from them in considerable detail. He has also given approval for the reproduction of the marvellous Tom Pennethorne Water colours in his possession, of East Cowes Castle, Norris Castle and West Cowes.

There are two major contributors of photographs to this work. Firstly, The Hon. Mrs Villiers, a descendant of the Vereker Family, the former owners of East Cowes Castle, has very kindly given me permission to publish from the family photograph collection of 1884, this inclusion has greatly enhanced the work. Secondly, the Royal Commission on the Historic Monuments of England has been an invaluable source of help and material, and I must mention Liz Churchman and Anne Woodward from the Fortress House Archives at Saville Row and Victoria Joyce from the Acton Aerial Photography Branch for their sustained help. The photographic Library of the R.C.H.M.E. is vast and a first stop for would be researchers in this subject.

On the Isle of Wight I must thank Mrs Frances Few of Yarmouth and Mr and Mrs Robert Few of Lower Hamstead for their kind assistance and permission to reproduce various pictures. At East Cowes, Roy Brinton, Connie Tennant and Rosetta Brading for more photographs and local information. Also Mr C Webster from the County Archives for searching out the information regarding Nash's land purchase at East Cowes and for the missing details of Heathfield.

My team of course deserve special thanks, Michael Sibbick for his series of drawings taken from the best information I could give him and his deliberations. Alan Hull for the extensive photography, a fraction of which is used here, Keith Woolley for art work, plans and presentation and Danny Payne for his digital reconstruction of the East Cowes Castle floor plans. To Jackie and Dawn for their typing skills and ability to decipher my writing.

For their forbearance and assistance throughout with presentation and selection of type styles, I must thank Edward and Doreen Porter of Business by Design. To David and Alison Harvey of The Cannon Press my appreciation is due for their enthusiasm and quality of production.

Finally to my wife and family who have lived with me and John Nash for the last months.

Ian Sherfield
Lynsted,Kent.
Spring 1994.

ACKNOWLEDGEMENTS FOR ILLUSTRATIONS

Acknowledgements are due to the undermentioned for permission to reproduce the photographs and drawings listed.

Mr Peter Laing :	Colour Plates 1,2, B/W Plates 4,20i,20ii,23,69
Mrs Frances Few :	Colour Plate 3, B/W Plate 71
Mr and Mrs Robert Few:	Colour Plate 4
The Royal Commission on the Historic Monuments of England :	
	B/W Plates 7,10,11,28,34,35,36,38,39, 40,41,42, 43,44,45,46,47,50, 51,60A,60B
© RCHME Crown Copywright	
Mr Roy Brinton :	B/W Plates 8,9,15,19i.,29,49
The Hon.Mrs Villiers :	B/W Plates 12,13,17,19ii,27,30,31,32,33
Isle of Wight College of Arts & Technology :	B/W Plate 26B
RAF/RCHME :	End papers, B/W Plate 37
© M.O.D. Crown Copywright	
Mrs Connie Tennant :	B/W Plate 48
Ordnance Survey/RCHME :	B/W Plate 52
© O.S. Crown Copywright	
Commission for Public Works in Ireland :	B/W Plates 63A,63B,64,66
Royal Institute of British Architects :	B/W Plates 65,67
Mr Michael Sibbick :	Figs 1,2,3,7,12,13, sketch page 54
Admiralty Hydrographic Office :	Fig 4
The Church Wardens of St.James, East Cowes:	B/W Plates 24,77
Medina Borough Council:	B/W Plate 68
Other B/W Plates from the Author's collection.	
©Crown Copywright :	Reproduced with the permission of the controller of Her Majesty's Stationery Office.

LIST OF ILLUSTRATIONS

COLOUR PLATES

1. East Cowes Castle from the West : 1815
2. Miniatures of Mary Anne Bradley and John Nash : c1798
3. East Cowes Castle from the south-east : 1815
4. East Cowes Castle from the north west: c1820

BLACK AND WHITE PLATES

End Papers (Front) East Cowes Castle Estate - south 1948
          (Back) East Cowes Castle Estate - north 1948

CHAPTER 1

1. Downton Castle : elevation
2. Downton Castle : setting
3. East Cowes Castle north-west front : c1808
4. Norris Castle : 1815
5. East Cowes Castle entrance front : c1826
6. East Cowes Castle north-west front : c1826
7. East Cowes Castle dining-room
8. East Cowes Castle drawing-room
9. East Cowes Castle library and octagon-room
10, East Cowes Castle garden long walk : 1935
11. East Cowes Castle kitchen garden conservatories : 1935
12. East Cowes Castle ornamental garden fountain : c1884
13. East Cowes Castle ornamental garden statue : c1884
14A. East Cowes Castle south-west front : c1824
14B. East Cowes Castle south-west front : c1831
15. East Cowes Castle conservatories
16. East Cowes Castle view from south-west : c1827
17. East Cowes Castle conservatory lawn entrance: c1884
18. Buckingham Palace : c1830
19i,19ii. East Cowes Castle gallery
20i,20ii. East Cowes Castle Accounts: 1835
21. North Lodge : 1820
22. Sandrock Hotel : c1834
23. Nash's Diary : 1835
24. The Sarcophagus of John Nash

CHAPTER 2

25. Shannon Castle : c1845
26A.Shannon Castle : c1845
26B.The clock mechanism from East Cowes Castle
27. East Cowes Castle conservatory: 1884
28. East Cowes Castle entrance front : 1911
29. East Cowes Castle entrance front south : c1911
30. East Cowes Castle view to the north : 1884
31. East Cowes Castle view to the south : 1884
32. East Cowes Castle regents room: 1884
33. East Cowes Castle garden: 1884
34. Southgate Lodge
35. East Cowes Castle approach from North Lodge : c1934
36. East Cowes Castle approach from Southgate Lodge : c1934

CHAPTER 3

37. Cowes: aerial view 1942
38. East Cowes Castle Entrance front : 1949
39. East Cowes Castle north-west front : 1949
40. East Cowes Castle view to the south : 1949
41. East Cowes Castle view to the north : 1949
42. East Cowes Castle view to the north-West : 1949
43. East Cowes Castle staircase tower : 1949
44. East Cowes Castle billiards-room : 1949
45. East Cowes Castle drawing-room : 1949
46. East Cowes Castle conservatory entrance : 1949
47. East Cowes Castle stable block : 1949
48. East Cowes Castle view from the south : c1958
49. East Cowes Castle view from the east : c1958
50. Southgate Lodge : c1964
51. North Lodge : c1964
52. Cowes aerial photograph : 1963
53. The Site today

CHAPTER 4

54. Luscombe Castle and groundfloor plan
55. Killymoon Castle and groundfloor plan
56. Garnstone Castle, front elevation
57. Childwall Hall, front elevation
58. Kilwaughter Castle and groundfloor plan
59. Ravensworth Castle and groundfloor plan

60A. Caerhays Castle, from the sea
60B. Caerhays Castle, entrance front
61.   West Grinstead Park and groundfloor plan
62.   Knepp Castle and groundfloor plan
63A. Lough Cutra Castle, from across the Lough
63B. Lough Cutra Castle, octagon Tower
64   Shanbally Castle, front elevation
65   Shanbally Castle elevation drawings
66   Shanbally Castle, entrance front
67.   Shanbally Castle groundfloor plan

CHAPTER 5

68. Northwood House
69. West Cowes : c1815
70. Nunwell House : c1834
71. Hamstead : c1835
72. Isle of Wight Institution : c1834
73. St Mildred's Church : c1816
74. Hillgrove & Trinity Church Bembridge : 1819
75. Guildhall Newport: c1834
76. Hippisley House : 1825
77. St.James's Church

FIGURES

1. John Nash c1827: from a portrait by Sir Thomas Lawrence.

CHAPTER 1

2. Castle House and plan
3. 29 Dover Street and plan
4. Cowes : Hydrographic Map of 1883
5. East Cowes Castle : groundfloor plan 1808
6. East Cowes Castle : groundfloor plan 1817
7. 14/16 Regent Street
8. Buckingham Palace plan : c1830
9. East Cowes Castle groundfloor plan 1835

CHAPTER 2

10. East Cowes Castle groundfloor plan 1949

CHAPTER 5

11. Isle of Wight Map : c1835
12. Lodge at Northwood Park
13. Hamstead and groundfloor plan c1806

BIBLIOGRAPHICAL ABBREVIATIONS

Barber (1845   T.Barber, *Pictuesque Illustrations of the Isle of Wight* **(1845)**

Davis (1960)   T.Davis, *The Architecture of John Nash* **(1960)**

Davis (1966)   T.Davis, John Nash: *The Prince Regent's Architect* **(1966)**

Farington Typescript   The Diary of Joseph Farington, 1793-1821; typescript copy in the Print Room, British Museum

Mansbridge (1991)   M.Mansbridge, *John Nash: A Complete Catalogue* **(1991)**

Nash (1832)   The Diary of John Nash **1832** ⎱ Nash Diaries in the possession
Nash (1835)   The Diary of John Nash **1835** ⎰ of Mr Peter Laing

Nash Papers ⎱   Papers in the possession of Mr Peter Laing, papers formerly
Pennethorne Papers ⎰ **(1935)** in the possession of James Pennethorne Esq.

RCHME   Royal Commission on the Historic Monuments of England

RIBA Cat   Catalogue of the Drawings Collection of the Royal Institute of British Architects

Sale Cat (1835)   Catalogue of the valuable architectural and miscellaneous library, prints and drawings,of the late John Nash, Esq. Sold by Evans of Pall Mall, **15-20 July 1835**.
Copies in British Museum and Soane Museum.

Statement (1829)   J.Nash, *A Statement* **(1829)**. Copy in the possession of Mr Peter Laing.

Summerson (1935)   J.Summerson, *John Nash: Architect to King George IV* **(1935; 2nd Edition 1949)**

Summerson (1980)   Sir J.Summerson,*The Life and Works of John Nash: Architect* **(1980)**

1828 Report   Report from the Select Committee on the Office of Works, BPP **1828**

1829 Report   Report from the Select Committee on Crown Leases, BPP **1829**

1831 Report   Second Report of the Select Committee on Windsor Castle and Buckingham Palace, BPP **1831**

Introduction

Very clever, good humoured, a sincere friend, civil, odd, a great coxcomb or a galloping raconteur, John Nash was many things to many people during his life time and such was the diverse nature and success of his work. Nevertheless, coincident with his first visit to the Isle of Wight during 1793 until his enforced retirement in 1830, Nash placed himself and remained in the forefront of British architecture. Initially travelling the length and breadth of the Kingdom completing private commissions and public works producing a range of buildings that no other contemporary architect could claim to have accomplished.

Such was the energy and persuasion of the man that he was able to open up Regents Park with some of the most innovative work of the nineteenth century, design and build an Oriental palace on the south coast of unparalleled richness, radically replan the west end of London providing a thoroughfare that would grace any city and finally, at the age of seventy-three to embark on the reconstruction of Buckingham House in an attempt to provide a palace of state proportions from a blueprint intended for a royal residence.

East Cowes Castle, is therefore, just one small chapter in the story of this extraordinary man and is as a consequence, impossible to present without considering the circumstances that made its creation and development possible and something of the architect's life while resident there.

The Seat of John Nash Esq was demolished thirty years ago: it had dominated the eastern skyline of Cowes for one hundred and sixty years.

1

1793 - 1835 : THE NASH EPOCH

i Associations

The career of John Nash was gathering momentum, following a disastrous speculative building enterprise in Bloomsbury, when he first visited the Isle of Wight in 1793. He had completed several significant private commissions in Wales, designed and built several cast iron bridges and was advising on major public works which ultimately were to come under his charge. Furthermore he was about to be initiated in a new order of architecture that was to secure the success of his future.

Nash had successfully remodelled a house called Hafod in the beautiful countryside of Cardiganshire for William Johnes, a man of rare talents and romantic inclinations and a taste for adventure within the arts. The remodelling undertaken, a new front, reordered windows and the building of a library and conservatory was, by 1794 the most interesting and adventurous he had attempted. More importantly it was undertaken in very close collaboration with the client. This in turn introduced Nash to Johnes's circle of friends, two of which were to become of primary importance to his future, not as patrons but by way of introducing Nash to their philosophy of 'the picturesque'. This was the reappraisal of the world of landscape gardening and its relationship with architecture, into a new poetic movement towards the co-ordination of building and natural surroundings. The first of the circle was Richard Payne Knight of Downton who was a relative of Johnes's wife, moreover his wife was Ursula Nash who may have been a relative of our subject. The other friend of Johnes's was Uvedale Price who was Payne Knight's neighbour at Foxley in Hertfordshire, Nash would have derived benefit from this association of rich scholarly romantic landowners with their theories towards the harmonic association of 'the picturesque'.

One other circumstance that established Nash firmly within this coterie occurred during 1795, when he was commissioned to design and build a mansion for Uvedale Price, upon the rocks of the rugged coastal locality of Aberystwyth. This was to be Nash's first attempt at 'the picturesque' developing his own ideas from the philosophy. The result, known as Castle House, *figure 2*, was a symmetrical triangular Gothic house, [1] harmonised with its environment. However, here perhaps was the inexperienced Nash at work as although the unusual house approached the ideal, its symmetrical design did not fully achieve the aesthetics as set by the protagonists and was more reminiscent of an exercise in earlier eighteenth century Classical architecture.

Nash did not perhaps appreciate that this concept had been captured in full by Payne Knight as early as 1774 when he rebuilt his house as a castle, not in the traditional symmetrical style but with disorder of turrets, towers and battlements, such that its exterior was deliberately unco-ordinated. Not a large house overall, but perfectly positioned overlooking the wooded valleys of the Teme, combining the element of irregularity in tune with natural surroundings. The interior however was quite different, Classical elegance in a series of well proportioned rooms.

1 - Royal Worcester produced a china model of the triangular house.

CASTLE HOUSE, ABERYSTWYTH c.1796-7

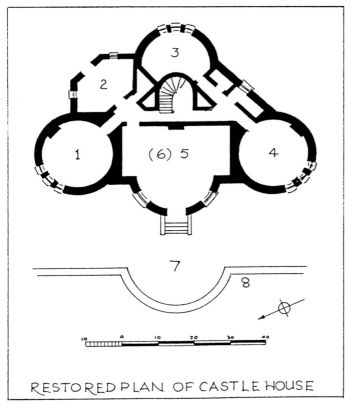

RESTORED PLAN OF CASTLE HOUSE

SUGGESTED ROOM NAMES

1	LIBRARY	5	SALOON
2	HALL	6	DRAWING ROOM (ABOVE)
3	KITCHEN	7	TERRACE
4	DINING ROOM	8	SEA

CASTLE HOUSE ABERYSTWYTH

the symmetrical house on the rocks built by Nash for Uvedale Price C1796 – 1797.

FIGURE 2.

East Cowes Castle

At what date Nash became acquainted with Downton is not known, he may have remodelled the octagonal tower there between 1782-1805[1] but it is more likely that this was carried out after Castle House. The impression that it made on him however, was said to be great and between Castle House and East Cowes, we see Nash's change in his interpretation of 'the picturesque'. Downton Castle had become the *avant-courier* of Nash's cycle of Neo-Gothic castle-houses.

There was one other person who was instrumental in promoting Nash's change in approach and who made a major contribution to his success from this time. This was Humphrey Repton, another exponent of 'the picturesque' and at this time a moderately successful landscapist.

Like Nash, Repton was acquainted with Richard Payne Knight and although sympathetic to the principles of 'the picturesque' had defended their criticism of Capability Brown's 'clump and belt and could have been made in London by contract and erected on the spot' philosophy, considering himself as the embodiment of Brown's ideals, but romantically adapting them towards the less formal picturesque.

During 1796 Paul Cobb Methuen of Corsham Court wished to enlarge the property to incorporate the whole of the family treasures, part of which were housed in their London mansion. Corsham was a large Elizabethan symmetrical house already enlarged by Capability Brown in 1769. Methnuen first consulted James Wyatt, a contemporary of Nash's from their articled days at the Sir Robert Taylor office, for his proposals to enlarge the house and Humphrey Repton to improve the landscaping. Repton was by this time hailed as the new 'Capability'. He then dismissed Wyatt and appointed Nash who was already known to the client and at Corsham, the two professionals first combined to simultaneously enrich the landscape and the architecture within it.

Nash and Repton were of similar age and background when Corsham was started and from this enterprise an unofficial partnership developed. Repton making the introductions and producing his famous 'Red Books' many of which survive, depicting the existing and proposed elevations and vistas via a hinged overlay system. Nash taking on the design and building, from his office, initially in Wales and subsequently in London. The partnership was unfortunately to end with bitter re-criminations on Repton's side over Nash's apparent lack of recognition of Repton's son, John Adey who worked in Nash's office. He was to leave the office in 1799 as a result of this disagreement but was superseded by his brother George Stanley Repton, who produced his famous R.I.B.A. and Brighton sketch books and was to remain with Nash until sometime after 1820. However, during the four or five years the Nash-Repton partnership survived, it established both men professionally within the circle of the most wealthy and influential estate owners, who wished to build, remodel or landscape their demesnes.

Against this background and although Corsham was to prove a disaster for Nash, due to poor building quality and a long term dry rot problem, business flourished and by 1798, when the story of East Cowes begins, we see Nash as a tremendously successful and wealthy country house architect, in partnership with Repton, undertaking the most prestigious and lucrative commissions of the day.

---

1 - *Mansbridge 1991 (P37) discusses the possibility of Nash having carried out work at Downton*

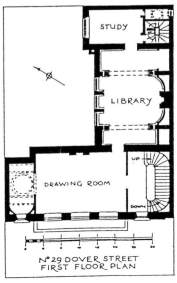

N° 29 DOVER STREET
FIRST FLOOR PLAN

STUDY

LIBRARY

DRAWING ROOM

UP

DOWN

29 DOVER STREET LONDON.

Nash's pretentious house overlooking Hay Hill.

17   **FIGURE 3.**

At this point, there is a suspicion that not withstanding the measure of Nash's success and forthcoming royal patronage, that he enjoyed a life style and wealth far beyond his station. However, during 1797 he took a speculative lease on a property in Dover Street, London, No 28, with a vacant plot adjacent and by the end of that year had moved in. He immediately commenced the building of No 29 and by the end of 1798 had completed for himself a visually impressive mansion, allowing the re-leasing of No 28. His new property was more extensive than every other in the street, with a three bay colonnade commanding the vista up Hay Hill, it was the veritable residence of a man of importance, *figure 3.*

The real motive behind this development was that on 17 December 1798, Nash took a new wife, Mary Anne Bradley, whose father was a partner in a firm of Coal Merchants, John and Robert Bradley of Abington Street, Westminster. The Bradleys originally came from Worcestershire and were related by marriage to the Worcestershire Pennethornes, a name that was to become an important part of the Nash's lives at East Cowes [1]. There is a suggestion at this juncture that Nash's new wife may have been a mistress of the then Prince of Wales, and this could have been the reason for his great wealth and subsequent royal patronage, the matter was however complicated many years later, when the Duke of Wellington whilst acting as executor to the late King George IV, is believed to have destroyed most of the personal papers relating to the circumstances.

To sum up, in 1798 we see Nash remarried, the occupier of a prestigious mansion in one of the best parts of London, exhibiting a work for the Prince of Wales at the Royal Academy but more significantly, purchasing a site for a country seat on the Isle of Wight.

1 - Davis 1966 (P57-59) Terrence Davis discusses the Nashes relationship with the Pennethorne children

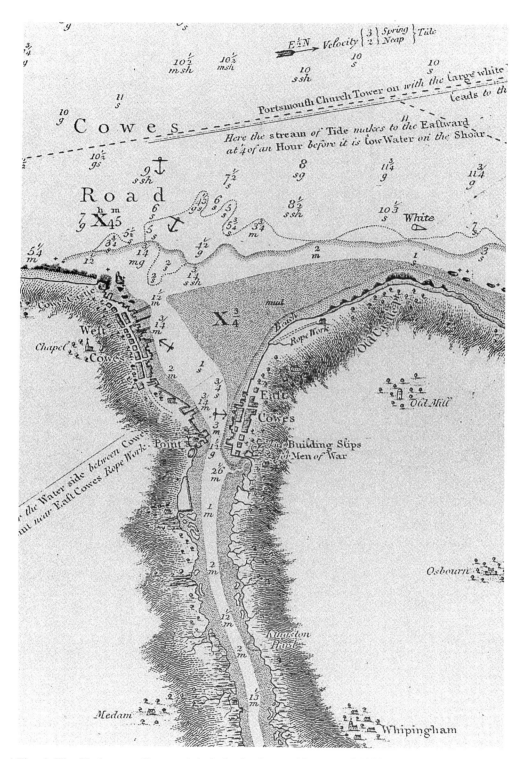

Fig. 4. The Harbour at Cowes: Admiralty hydrographic map of 1883

ii Building The Castle

Throughout the period 1793 to 1798, Nash made several journeys to the Isle of Wight to visit an old friend from London, Admiral McBride, who had an address in Cowes. He may at this time also have been introduced to George Ward, the rich financier and landowner who lived in the locality for whom Nash was to ultimately complete several commissions. No visitor to the Island, at that time, could fail to be captivated by the beauty of the northern approaches from across the Solent, the tip of the Island quite hilly and in the late eighteenth century, heavily wooded, with the terrain rising quite suddenly from the shore and bisected by the wide tidal Medina. The little hamlets of East and West Cowes populated the waters edge and served the local communities of a few hundred souls from fishing, farming, boat building and rope making. On the surrounding hills there were a few villas and large country estates notably the Debourne and Bellevue Estates on the west and Osborne and Barton Manor Estates on the east.

The area was mapped in 1783 and *figure 4* depicts the natural sheltered harbour of Cowes, this being the only berthing facility for a ship of any size at that time for the Island. Nash would have had ample time to appreciate this scene as the mail packet ship from Southampton to Cowes would not possess motive power, steam power was not introduced generally until around 1821. There was however a mail coach service from London completing the 76 miles with reasonable expedition, connecting with the shipping service across the Solent.

One can perhaps imagine Nash with his developing commercial success and leanings toward 'the picturesque' contemplating his vision of a country seat on the Isle of Wight whilst making journeys to Cowes. Evident in that during 1798 he purchased around 30 acres of land including two messuages, two cottages, two barns, three stables, a ruined windmill, arable pasture and meadow, 5 acres of woodland and an acre of furze and heath, from Lambert Fochier de Lambert at East Cowes in the parish of Whippingham. The estate overlooking the hamlet and the woodland and meadow sloping abruptly towards the riverbank and shore. Upon the peak, the remains of an old windmill, providing the focal point above the locality and the perfect setting for the placement of architecture within 'the picturesque'.

Why the Isle of Wight? One might consider the implications of a French invasion during 1798, the war with France was not going well and although the Island was heavily garrisoned it did not then possess any significant defence against seaborne attack and may well have figured as a stepping stone in Napoleon's territorial intentions. But the Isle of Wight with its tree clad hillsides, healthy environment and sufficient remoteness was the ideal locality for the emergent Nash to supplement his ostentatious London mansion. Furthermore no less a person than Lord Henry Seymour had acquired the adjoining estate at Norris and had commissioned Nash's old adversary James Wyatt, the Surveyor-General to build him a castle so, at a stroke, Nash was to place himself within a distinguished and fashionable locality.

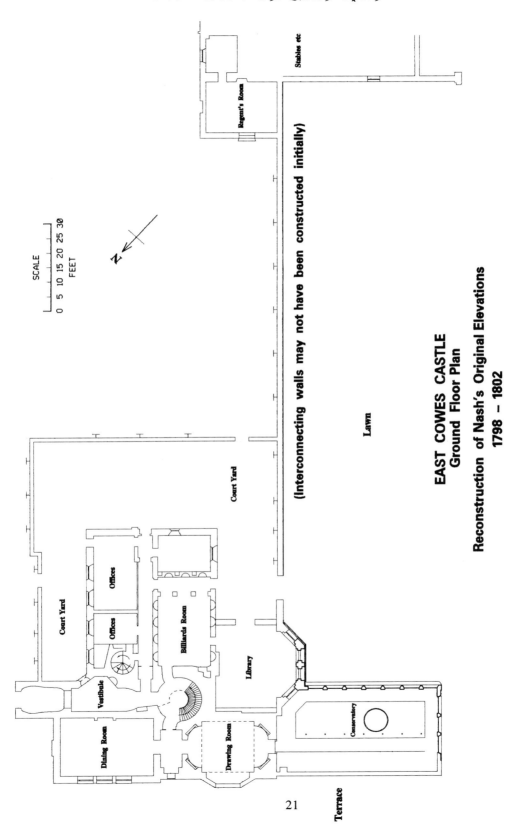

SCALE

0 5 10 15 20 25 30

FEET

N

(Interconnecting walls may not have been constructed initially)

Stables etc

Regent's Room

Court Yard

Lawn

Court Yard

Offices

Offices

Billiards Room

Vestibule

Library

Dining Room

Drawing Room

Conservatory

Terrace

EAST COWES CASTLE
Ground Floor Plan

Reconstruction of Nash's Original Elevations
1798 – 1802

FIGURE 5

The site that Nash had so perfectly selected was bordered to the east by the newly formed estate of Norris and to the south by the Georgian estate of Osborne, at this time owned by the Blatchford family. To the west it was bounded by the ancient estate of East Shamblers and to the north by the hamlet of East Cowes and the grounds of the estate of Slatwoods. The East Cowes to Newport high road provided the dividing line between the Nash's new estate, Norris and Osborne and the access to his intentions a little way up from the harbour.

It would seem that work started almost immediately after the purchase of the estate, confirming that Nash had long fostered proposals for his country seat and by 1800 he had purchased a further 39 acres[1] from the adjacent Slatwoods Estate. The newly fashionable castle-house style popularised by Nash, at Aberystwyth, was the order and by 1802 the first stage of work was completed and ready for the Nashes occupation.

The result of Nash's first plan provided a modest country house depicted in Cooke's engraving [2] published in 1808, of the north west elevation of the building. A house of Georgian proportions, similar in size to Luscombe, which Nash was building from 1800 and of Gothic design. *Figure 5* is a reconstruction of the ground floor plan at this stage, which, indicates a strangely unco-ordinated series of rooms around the central staircase tower which was possibly the base of the old windmill. The dining-room with sash windows, decorated with labels and the drawing room with its spiky bay window, would have enjoyed panoramic views of the Solent and mainland beyond. The expanse of masonry stretching in a westerly direction was the rear crenellated wall of the conservatory. The building was topped overall with battlements and accordingly received the fashionable addition of 'Castle'. The large square tower to the south may have been a separate building at this stage, the architect initially recalling aspects of Downton.

Nash did not long content himself with a country retreat of this scale and as inspiration or gathering wealth allowed he systematically extended and remodelled the whole building, implementing initially perhaps the more successful features of like country house commissions. A further incentive was the completion of his neighbour's new castle at Norris, just one thousand yards distant . Norris had been completed by 1805, plain Norman stone architecture, with impressive views of the Solent but more importantly visually impressive to travellers rounding the tip of the Island, and making the obvious comparisons.

Co-incident with early stages of development at East Cowes, during 1806, Nash aquired his second Island estate, when he purchased the manor of Ningwood from William Chamberlaine, situated five miles south-west of Cowes, the estate extending to the Solent foreshore. Nash paid around £30,000 for the property which included the tiny hamlet of Hamstead, perched on a high down between the Newport to Yarmouth road and the coast, enjoying elevated views across the Solent from the New Forest to Southampton. The hamlet lodge Nash converted into a picturesque style manor-house incorporating a round tower and thatched roof. This he used initially as a shooting box, farmed the surrounding land and installed brick ovens and lime kilns, served by a light railway. Nash's work at Hamstead deserves further consideration and will be revisited in Chapter 5.

1 - *Of the land purchased in 1800 some 18½ acres at Mount Sylvan was sold or leased on, as the estate area in Nash's time was around 50 acres.*
2 - *W Cooke, New Picture of The Isle of Wight.*

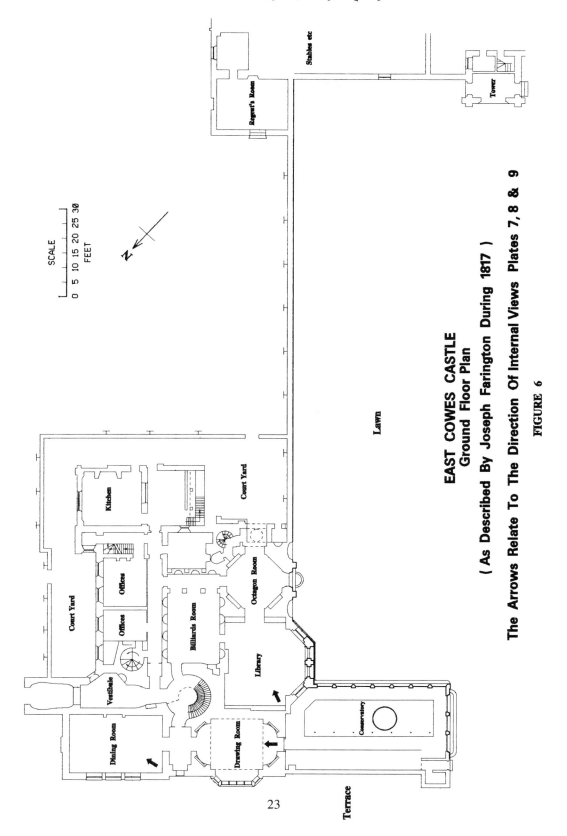

SCALE

0 5 10 15 20 25 30

FEET

N

Stables etc

Regent's Room

Tower

Lawn

Court Yard

Kitchen

Court Yard

Offices

Offices

Octagon Room

Billiards Room

Vestibule

Library

Dining Room

Drawing Room

Conservatory

Terrace

EAST COWES CASTLE
Ground Floor Plan

(As Described By Joseph Farington During 1817)

The Arrows Relate To The Direction Of Internal Views Plates 7, 8 & 9

FIGURE 6

By 1814 Nash's professional life had advanced from that of a country house architect to that of a major planner and developer. Regents Park was in progress and the Royal Pavilion at Brighton and Regent Street redevelopment were on his horizon, work at East Cowes however, continued unabated. A square tower constructed on the western end of the conservatory, a new bay window for the drawing-room and a new floor above with matching bartizans and new oriel windows for the room above the dining-room. A large square tower topped with a smaller square tower to the south, a massive octagonal with adjacent octagonal staircase tower and another square tower to the south west and interconnecting crenellated walling. The square, octagonal and round towers and turrets, the arcaded and castellated loggias producing somewhat variable but complimentary elevations. The machionated detail, the square and round headed windows, the pointed gothic arches and the expansive masonary combining to produce the illusion of a fortified Tudor mansion. Incorporated within this design however, were all the refinements of a much later domesticated manor house of grand scale.

The masonry was of hard stone[1] coursed rubble well executed, with shaped stone cappings and incised rendered part elevations, further enhancing the *ensemble*. The rustication and bold shapes combining to accord dramatic architecture within a beautiful elevated setting.

The centre piece octagonal tower added by 1811 is worth particular mention, approximately seventy-five feet high with the adjoining staircase tower protruding some fifteen feet above, contained four elaborate rooms all with differing window arrangements. These windows incorporated Nash's favourite neat folding shutters which were completely concealed within the window embrasures. Accessed by the circular stairs in the staircase tower, the stair segments were of cut stone, landed within the inner course of tower masonry. A series of hexagonal iron bars provided the central spine through the segment tips. There were ninety-nine steps of about eight inches rise in the tower and the flag staff platform was reached from the top of the main octagonal tower. Nash favoured and pioneered the use of iron in his construction and various roof support members at East Cowes were made of the material, as were the support members that were later to cause controversy in the construction at Buckingham Palace.

There was a plaque set into the wall within the staircase tower inscribed:

> **EAST COWES CASTLE**
> **DESIGNED AND BUILT**
> **BY**
> **JOHN NASH**
> **1798**

The striking exterior of East Cowes Castle was matched by an equally elaborate interior, photographed during the early part of this century and so nearly as in Nash's time we can do no better than retrace the visit made during 1817 by Joseph Farington [2] who on a fine September morning presented his card at the lodge and was told that he and his party might see the house and grounds.

Figure 6 indicates the scale of the house in 1817 and the direction of the internal views described.

---

1 - *The source of this material was probably local quarries*
2 - *Joseph Farington R.A. Noted Diarist of The Day*

Entering at the porch, which then projected considerably in advance of the main building, Nash may have originally intended this as *a porte cochère* which was a feature of many of his country houses, the Faringtons passed down a short corridor to the rather dull lop-sided vestibule and thence into the staircase tower, with its fluted walls, scaley dome, foliated gilt boss, suspended chandelier and prominent S balusters in the staircase rail. From here the servant 'very civilly shewed us into the dining-room, in which a table was very genteelly set for dinner for seven persons. This room was ornameted with several pictures - views of Houses designed by Mr Nash.'

The chief beauty of the dining-room was its fine cavetto cornice; the cove itself was vertically fluted and below was a tiny *motif* of curtains and tassels painted in red and gold and above was an ovolo with scaley enrichment. The ceiling was covered with a fine early nineteenth century paper. The black marble fireplace was set off with brass ornaments.

'The servant then told us,' continues Farington 'we might pass through the opposite room the drawing-room, in which was Mr Nash with company, all of whom were seated when we entered, and we only passed through the middle of the room to the conservatory. Mr Nash bowed'.

The occasion of meeting a distinguished architect at his country seat with no more acknowledgement than a bow seems rather contrived, as Nash must have known Farington quite well from his association with the Royal Academy. At this stage Farington presented the servant with two shillings 'with which he appeared pleased'.

The room which Farington had politely to pass through in which Mr Nash and company were present was of the period of the Paris Directoire. The curved end bays had flat ceilings at a lower level, and recesses lined with mirrors. The ceiling, raised on a cavetto cornice, with gilt anthemion was delicately ornamented, and the white marble fireplace had a pair of Egyptian figures supporting the mantle.

From the conservatory they passed to the library 'a handsome room well stored with books'. The library ceiling was a fulsome mixture of Gothic and acanthus, painted red, blue, green and gold, the fireplace was similar to that of the drawing-room.

Beyond the library, at the base of the octagon tower was a room with a radial fluted circular ceiling carried by eight arches and ornamented with a grey marble fireplace. The billiard room next door was a charming pastiche, from the later work of Sir John Soane, with a series of ten small domes in its roof surrounding a lay light.

Farington's tour of inspection ended at this point[1] but he returned in October 1821 after receiving 'a pressing invitation to visit Mr Nash at his mansion near East Cowes and stay some days with him'. On this occasion Farington recorded the vista through the conservatory, the drawing-room and the dining-room. Nash gave a conducted tour of his prolific kitchen garden and narrated to the diarist the story of his life.

1 - *The Diaries of Joseph Farington, Vol III P143* (*September 6, 1817*)

East Cowes Castle

Sometime after Farington's second visit Nash commenced the construction of what was perhaps the *tour de force* of the whole castle, the long conservatory. Nash may have gained inspiration from his professional activities at the time, as he was involved in the detail planning of Regent Street, however the result at East Cowes was a south-west facing claustral setting of nineteen Gothic arches [1] terminated by the octagonal tower and complemented by eight similar arches of the earlier conservatory facing south-west. The development and scale of this elevation can be seen from *figure 9* and the Brannon Engravings published 1824 and 1831 indicating that the arches of the long conservatory may have been unglazed initially or fitted with removable glazed panels, a feature used at Luscombe some years earlier

Topped with battlements, the long conservatory provided the appropriate link between the main body of the house and the large square tower to the south known as the Regents room. There is however, no record of the Regent having stayed there and Nash referred to it in his diary as 'The room at the end of the conservatory'. Nash stocked his conservatory with many varieties of exotic plants of the day. There were ornamental ponds and fountains and statuettes and the walkways through the conservatory were inlaid with mosaics.

The ambience of Nash's creativity is captured in a fragment of text discovered on the reverse of a framed print. 'The new conservatory is on a magnificent scale, and of very grand design, constituting a most splendid improvement to the general imposing effect of this noble edifice. The collection of rare and valuable exotics is at present ample, and large accessions are daily making - the grounds fall favourably with gentle undulations to the water and are happily interspersed with several and flourishing plantations; while the immediate foreground of the castle is enriched by an exquisite display of magnolias and other choice flowering shrubs that are rarely equalled for luxuriance of growth in the open air. In the decoration of the grounds Mr. Nash has envinced the greatest taste and judgement, giving them an appearance of much more extent that they really possess '.

John Summerson when visiting the castle during 1933 records that 'any planting Repton [1] may have done has by this time grown somewhat too luxuriant, and that today the shrubberies are tangled and unkempt but the grounds still display contrived variety and immense beauty. The library and octagon room look across the lawn to a rich jungle of trees, rhododendrons and azaleas, growing at the bottom of a grassy slope, falling away from the lawn and covered in springtime with primroses and daffodils. Within the jungle are winding paths, groves and ponds. From the drawing and dining-rooms the prospect is sloping parkland, with the sea beyond. The entrance side is different again; here the architecture, wearing a baronial frown, is framed with vast elms and beeches'.

A little apart from the castle was a formal garden with a fountain and large elliptical ornamental pond surrounded with many varieties of exotic and sub tropical shrubs.Further south was the walled kitchen garden and orangery, of which, Nash was very proud. It was formed on the slope of a hill and consisted of five broad terraces, built of brick with slate floors under the soil. The slate 'prevents any but good earth lodging at the roots of the fruit trees. The roots not being able to penetrate the floor, shoot out horizontally'. So Nash told Farington, such that the fruit 'is excellent and plentiful', and surpassed that of his neighbours. The garden remained much as photographed in 1935, the conservatories only having been replaced.

In Nash's time there was one official entrance to the castle from the East Cowes to Newport high road, just above the harbour at Springhill. Nash marked this entrance to his estate with a charming *cottage orné,* known as North Lodge, it was one of several he designed in the locality and similar to one of the series of designs that Nash so successfully employed at Blaise Hamlet and in numerous other country house commissions.

1 - *There is a detail drawing of the conservatory arches within the East Cowes Castle archive at the RCHME*
2 - *Repton whilst in partnership with Nash may have contributed the design of the Castle grounds between the years 1798 - 1800*

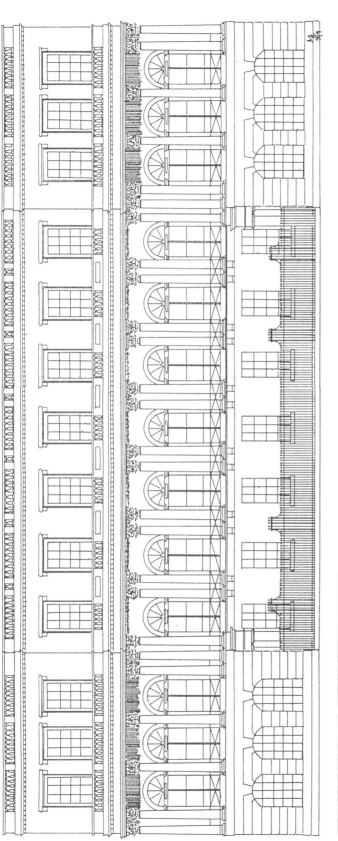

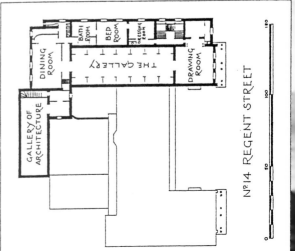

14 /16 REGENT STREET LONDON.

**The double Mansion designed by Nash
and shared with his cousin Mr. John Edwards.**

FIGURE 7.

GALLERY OF
ARCHITECTURE

DINING
ROOM

BATH
ROOM

BED
ROOM

DRESSING
ROOM

THE GALLERY

DRAWING
ROOM

Nº 14 REGENT STREET

0   50   100   150

East Cowes was therefore just as perfect a Country Seat as Nash could conceive. It was no mere retreat from the pressures of his metropolitan world, more his principal place of residence from which he enjoyed and maintained the status of a country gentlemen from 1802 until his death in 1835. It is perhaps difficult to envisage how Nash could be one of the most successful architects in the land and via his royal patronage, have access to one of the largest purses in the Kingdom and yet be absent from London for significant periods of time. Nash did of course have extensive offices at 29 Dover Street from 1798 to 1821 and from 1821 to 1834, at the magnificent double mansion at 14/16 Regent Street, *figure 7*. He designed and built this house as part of the Regent Street development which he shared with his mysterious cousin and business associate John Edwards. He also had extensive offices at the castle from which he could direct his business interests, dispatching both instructions and designs throughout the land. But succeed he did, as both *distingué* host and *premier* architect.

The reason Nash was able to manage his affairs in this way was his strategy towards intermixing of business and pleasure. He was never a man to draw a hard line between social and business life, he enjoyed combining them and derived considerable advantage from doing so. Consequently both Nash and his wife Mary Anne, were eager hosts and the castle was rarely without visitors. The shortest of associations with the Nashes could bring the most unconventional of invitations, pressing but kindly, an example of such exists. It is to Robert Gray, Keeper of the Prince Regent's privy purse, who had apparently been ill:-

> *Allow me to repeat my invitation to you and Mrs Gray ... we have pony carts and an Irish jaunting car a close carriage and a very gentle horse for you to ride - hot and cold bathing, salt or fresh in the house -civil waiting and an attentive landlord and landlady - fine sea breezes and gravelled roads - where can you find a more commodious Inn? Try it and believe me with a due sense of your kindness for which I am your debtor - My Dear Sir.*
> *faithfully yours*
> *J. Nash*

Pressing indeed and unconventional but such invitations were not only open to important people. Assistants and pupils from the London office were also welcome at the castle where they had the opportunity to mix with all manner of people, politicians, artists, lawyers and actors, with the liberty to ride, shoot and swim and take full advantage of the recreational pursuits that the Island provided. In the evenings to listen to music or play cards or take the evening air in the beautiful castle grounds.

1817 was an *annus mirabilis* at East Cowes for on July 13 the Prince Regent came over from Brighton to dine at the castle. Four hundred soldiers from Parkhurst barracks formed a guard of honour. In August of the same year he arranged to return and his chéf spent several days at the castle in preparation and quantities of provisions were brought over from Southampton. He then changed his mind and the Nashes sent out hasty invitations to the Island gentry. One hundred and twenty of them arrived. They danced, sat down at midnight to what should have been a royal banquet and afterwards danced till dawn.

In September the Prince was again at Cowes, he was becoming fond of sailing in the fashionable resort and that same year the *Royal George*, a yacht of 320 tons was built for him at Deptford. At about this time he bought from Nash's neighbour at West Cowes, George Ward, a house on the Parade, situated to the east of Cowes Castle.

Lord Henry of Seymour of Norris Castle was host to the Prince for his next visit to the Island in 1819. Lord Henry was not noted for high living but on this occasion we are told the event was attended with 'circumstances of unusual conviviality'. During this visit John Edwards, Nash's cousin, was invited with the party taken aboard the royal yacht, doubtless as a favour to the architect. There was yet another royal visit in September 1820, this time by the newly ascended but as yet uncrowned monarch. Once again Nash, George Ward and others of the Island gentry dined aboard the *Royal George*.

From one of the later years of the Regency an unsent invitation card[1] has survived the virtual total destruction of Mrs Nash's papers after her death in 1851.

> *Mr and Mrs Nash*
> *request the honour of*
> *Lady Melville and Family's*
> *Company to a Déjeuné and Fête*
> *on the Lawn at East Cowes Castle*
> *at 2 o'Clock on & in Commemoration*
> *of The Prince Regent's Birth Day*

Nash's guests of the castle were drawn from many professions, lawyers, politicians, artists but just one architect. He was C R Cockerell, son of S P Cockerell of Sezincote fame (1803) and who had been a fellow trainee of Nash's. The younger Cockerell and Nash having a special liking and admiration for one another. The Artist J M W Turner was a guest of the Nashes on more than one occasion and during his visit in the Autumn of 1827 he painted pictures for his host. In all Turner is believed to have painted nine pictures whilst staying at East Cowes. 'Cowes Regatta', 'Sailing on the River', and 'The Music Room of the Castle' were given to Nash and are now on view at the Tate Gallery. Other compositions included 'Shipping off East Cowes Headland', 'Shipping in the Solent' and 'Yacht Racing in the Solent'.

There were also gifts to favoured visitors to the castle. During 1826 Nash commissioned the local engraver and printer, George Brannon to produce for him a specially bound limited edition of six views of the castle. The resulting prints measuring approximately 13 inches by 8 inches are significantly larger than the famous engravings that Brannon produced of Isle of Wight scenes during the years 1815 - 1840.

The delights of East Cowes Castle, its leafy estate and the hospitable ways of its master are chronicled in diaries, letters and memoirs of the time. At his country retreat Nash was seen at his most relaxed and companionable, merry, amusing, naive, a galloping raconteur who at seventy was likely to tell the same story twice. Very clever, odd, an amusing man, with a face like a monkey's but civil and good humoured to the greatest degree, were some of the recorded impressions, favourable and otherwise by his guests.

Farington's account[2] of his two day stay in the castle during 1821 relates to dinner parties on both days for which he gives table plans. On these occasions seated at the table with the Nashes were members of the Pennethorne family, Tom, Ann, James, Sarah and John the cousins of Mrs Nash.

1 - Nash Papers
2 - Farington Typescript

East Cowes Castle

As a consequence of this relationship each of the Pennethorne children benefited from the Nashes generosity and the quality of life, whilst living within the Nash ménage. Initially Tom was taken into Nash's office, he had a great artistic talent and had been given lessons at East Cowes by Turner, but died before he was twenty. His place was taken by his younger brother, James.

Ann meanwhile, became almost a daughter substitute to Mrs Nash at East Cowes, who having no children of her own, was in need of the companionship and help with the continual round of entertaining at the castle. In time, this provided for Ann exposure to the variety of male company ever present from which a good marriage might result. Nash, no doubt, had this is mind when he told Farington that he intended a legacy for her of £10,000. But marry she did not and an affair with a curate of Whippingham ended with him retreating over a matter of concience and taking up a successful career in education. Ann remained a companion to Mrs Nash until her death in 1851 and said of the old lady, when she was buried at St James's Church, that she was 'the kindest, best friend that anyone ever had'.

James Pennethorne, following in Tom's footsteps, gained professionally from the association. Initially perhaps, overshadowed by his more talented brother he was trained in the office, followed by two years in Pugin's drawing school, and finally two years study abroad, all at Nash's expense. During 1828 he became Nash's principle assistant, to whom, he resigned his practice in 1834. Eventually, through a series of administrative advances, became salaried architect to Queen Victoria's government, displaying great ability and retiring after a very full and distinguished career, with a Knighthood in 1869.

Of the other two Pennethorne children rather less is known, but John was given the very same opportunities to make a career in architecture, by Nash. After making his name as a scholar in Greek Architecture and producing the lengthy work, *The Geometry and Optics of Ancient Architecture* published in 1878, he retired to Hamstead. Sarah, an accomplished needlewoman remains in the background, but examples of her family tapestries exist as an acknowledgement of her talent. She also lived within the family circle at Hamstead. Anne (1800-83), Sarah (1803-90) and John (1808-88) are buried at Shalfleet, the church nearby Hamstead and James (1801-71) is buried at Highgate.

Promoted perhaps, by the exemplary provision for the Pennethore family, was the continuing rumour of an amorous relationship between Mrs Nash and the Regent. The circumstances unproven, explored in detail by others [1] , have little relevance here. There is no reason to suppose that life at East Cowes was anything but decorous and that the Nashes and their associates were well suited, it was unfortunate that their marriage bore no children, but there were many compensations, not least to see the successful development of their charges. The considerable fruits of Nash's success were of benefit to many.

In later years Nash did not indulge the excesses of life, his diaries tell us that he enjoyed outdoor pursuits and he was abstemious with the bottle, Punch was his occasional tipple. He normally retired early, so presumably the bulk of the entertaining was carried out by Mrs Nash and Ann Pennethorne. He told Benjamin West [1] that he could happily live in a single room having his books about him, rather a contrast to his life style within the ample mansions of East Cowes and Regent Street! To Farington he expressed a fatalistic indifference to his future. He could live or die. He could fall to low estate without repining; easily said perhaps by a man who had reached the very pinnacle of his profession. Nash had tasted failure in the past, he had taken large risks, lived very close the edge and was still doing so, the consequences were perhaps acceptable to him. Nash was never lacking in courage or resilience, these qualities would be tested in full once more, before the end.

1 - *Summerson 1980 C11 P151,152*
2 - *Benjamin West, American President of The Royal Academy*

1. East Cowes Castle from the west: reproduced from a water colour by Tom Pennethorne painted in 1815.

2. Miniatures of Mary Anne Bradley and John Nash at about the time of their marriage in 1798. The miniature of Mrs Nash is attributed to Anne Mee, the artist for the miniature of John Nash is unknown.

3. East Cowes Castle from the south-east : reproduced from a water colour by Tom Pennethorne painted in 1815.

4. East Cowes Castle from the north-west: reproduced from a water colour about 1820. Believed to have been drawn by James Pennethorne and painted by C Moore

iii The Palace

I t is appropriate to consider the last years of Nash's professional life from 1820, before returning once more to the quiet haven of East Cowes. John Nash was an architect of considerable standing at this time, a public figure, having almost completed the resplendent pavilion at Brighton and enjoying the success of his ongoing London improvements. At the forefront of British architecture, he was no longer content with country house or interesting public commissions, he was an architect of scale, his boundless optimism, talent and drive had carried him to greater things.

Success at this level brings enemies and Nash had his share. Through his somewhat speculative dealings and royal patronage, he was unpopular among his contemporaries having to some extent eclipsed their ambitions by virtue of his thrusting all embracing style. It came as no surprise therefore, when in 1821 John Soane, who was supposed to be responsible for royal palaces, was instructed by the Surveyor General to handover all plans relating to Buckingham House, to Nash. Soane who had previously exhibited a considerable design for a new palace at Constitution Hill at the Royal Academy and presupposed that any revisions considered for Buckingham House would be his responsibility, was told however, that Nash was the King's personal choice.

As early as 1819 the Regent had shown interest in rebuilding Buckingham House, which had long been in royal ownership, originally purchased by George III in 1762, but the only money available was £ 150,000 and as £450,000 was considered necessary to complete the scheme, so for six years a dormant interest it remained. Nash meantime was busy fitting out staterooms at St James Palace, and progressing his various designs for the continuing London improvements. During 1823 the King wished to recondition Windsor, Parliament agreed and voted £150,000 for the work. Nash and his contemporaries were invited to tender, but designs and costs varied widely and although both Nash and Smirke were called to explain their intentions the work was given to Wyatt.

A bill enabling the Crown lands revenues to be applied for the remodelling of Buckingham House was introduced to the House of Commons in June 1825. Nash had already examined the options and considered building on another site to be preferable, but failing to convince his Majesty of this, he advised that resiting the house higher up the garden in line with Pall Mall would be more appropriate. Nash felt that the lowness of the existing site and the northern aspect would convince the King. This was not so and the issue was raised in conversation with the King when Lord Farnborough was present. The King was adamant:

'Long, now remember, I tell Nash before you, at his peril ever to advise me to build a palace. I am too old to build a palace. If the public wish to have a palace, I have no objection to build one, but I must have a *pied-à-terre*. I don't like Carlton House standing in a street, and moreover I tell him that I will have it at Buckingham House; and if he pulls it down he shall rebuild it in the same place; there are early associations which endear me to the spot'.

So the issue was settled and by May 2 1825 even though the plans were 'not quite finished', and no model had been constructed, the proposals were rushed through without detail consideration. Work began before the bill was passed, and members of the House voted for the repair and improvements to Buckingham House, the cost of which 'might not be less than £200,000', not withstanding £150,000 had already been approved for Windsor the year before. This figure was immediately increased by £30,000 plus an additional £22,920 for laying out the grounds, a matter which appears to have been accepted with little or no concern.

Nash's first designs were quite original and contained good elemental features, these were however badly co-ordinated. A long block incorporating some of the fabric of the original building, containing the principal rooms and main central entrance. Columnised pavilions at the flanks and above each, an isolated attic. Behind the central portico, which was raised to roof level was a large dome over the semi circular bay of the garden elevation. Two wings extended eastward and terminated in lofty pedimented pavilions, a continuous Doric order at ground floor level provided the only unity.

Work proceeded but Nash was soon aware that his design was not a success, furthermore the dome, completely out of proportion, dominated the roof line of the main block from the park side, whereas his intention had been to provide a feature seen only from the garden side.

By October 1825, a moderate £20,635 had been expended, but during the following December the first signs of unrest were evident when the Surveyor General, in writing to the Treasury suggested Nash's 'improvidence' in awarding contracts at less favourable prices than had the Board. Nash responded claiming that a uniform reduction of 10% in all trades had been negotiated and that the cheapest of prices would not provide the necessary quality of workmanship.

By April 1826 £90,365 had been spent and Nash's estimate for completion to the next stage was £132,265 still within budget, but as the year crept on things were beginning to get badly out of hand. Unfortunately for Nash he was attempting to satisfy two masters, the King on one hand had no intention of compromising his requirements for the sake of an estimate. If an idea occurred to him he would immediately convey it to Nash and expect to see it implemented. Nash admitted that most of the royal instructions were verbal and 'whenever I saw him it generally happened that he ordered some alteration'. Nash therefore felt bound to follow his instructions to the letter, the Treasury on the other hand expected Nash's prudence throughout.

Consequently the expenditure rose rapidly from £252,000 to £350,000 but a windfall sum of £250,000 relating to the adjustments of claims on France, would seem to have been allocated uncharacteristically by the Treasury somewhat disguising the true picture. During February 1828 there was a change of Government and Wellington became Prime Minister. On or about this time Nash announced the King's intention to demolish and rebuild the wings and he went to see Wellington about the matter. Nash received a very cool reception and was told in no uncertain terms that 'it was no business of his; they might pull down as much as they liked' but Wellington was well aware of the situation and continued 'If you expect me to put my hand to any additional expense, I'll be damned if I will!' Wellington was not a man to condone extravagances and he was only too well aware of the King's excesses and the amount by which the original estimate had been exceeded. The scale of this figure became public knowledge after a Governmental Committee was convened to examine the expense of public buildings and Nash and his contemporaries, Soane, Smirke, Wyatville[1] and others were called to appear. Many of Nash's activities were reviewed but the scandal associated with the cost of Buckingham House was the main item on the agenda and although the blame could not be levelled at any single person, the Parliamentary report[2] did nothing to ease Nash's precarious situation.

1 - *Wyatville, previously Wyatt*
2 - *1828 Report*

1793 - 1835 : The Nash Epoch

With the advent of Wellington's Government, Gouldbourne had become Chancellor and before long he instructed Nash not to obey the King's orders without sanction of the Treasury. This made Nash's position intolerable as he was obliged to shelve work ordered by the King, but dared not tell him of the Treasury's instructions. Even so the Treasury's attempt to retard expenditure was not effective. Nash agreed to limit monthly expenditure to £10,000 but this simply delayed the work and increased the ultimate liabilities. The considered waste of public money was intolerable enough, but resentment increased when the unsightly wings began to take shape. They were eventually built up to the level of the main block at a cost of £50,000 and porticoes added to the ends.

Nash was by this stage ill at ease with the whole design and remarked 'I was not at first aware that the effect would have been so bad, but now I think any wings would take from the dignity of a palace... I am sorry to say I was disappointed myself with the effect of them'. The dome over the main block was a further subject of derision and Nash was heavily criticized for that 'common slop-pail turned up-side down'. The triumphal arch positioned between the two wings was to be constructed of Bath stone as was the remainder of the building, but it was decided that it should be of white marble, a considerably more expensive material. There had been insufficient stocks available in London, so Nash obtained the Treasury's sanction to purchase Ravaccione marble in Italy. Banished to the junction of Oxford Street and Park Lane when in 1847 all Nash's work was hidden behind the new block constructed between the two wings, it was to become known as The Marble Arch. The equestrian statue of George IV intended for its summit was eventually placed in Trafalgar Square.

Whatever the public perception of Buckingham House, The King, it would seem was delighted, he summoned his architect to Carlton House, 'Nash the State rooms you have made me are so handsome that I think I shall hold my Courts there'. Nash was dismayed and respectfully emphasised that the building had been designed as a royal residence and did not possess the necessary accommodation for affairs of Court. 'You know nothing of the matter', replied the King; 'it will make an excellent Palace, and Lord St Helens and myself have arranged the use of the several apartments'. So, at the King's command Buckingham House became Buckingham Palace and Nash's blue print for a royal residence became a metropolitan palace.

A thousand craftsmen laboured for its completion by the King's birthday in 1830 and as the autumn of 1829 wore on many of them were required to work until 10.00 pm by candle light in an attempt to complete the outstanding work. The unfinished building remained stark and empty and Nash's standing as a public figure and architect was at an all time low. Clearly events could not be allowed to continue but until the King's death at Windsor on 26 June 1830, affairs at the Palace would not draw to a close.

Concurrent with the earlier stages of work at Buckingham House, during 1827, Nash was actively involved with the redevelopment of Carlton House. The old building had become unsafe and a considerable source of royal revenue could be derived from the site. This subject was also one of the activities examined by The 1828 Select Committee, and Nash was asked, 'Who called on you to give your elevations for these works, to give the general plan for the buildings in Carlton House Gardens'. He replied, 'The probability is that I received the directions from the person whom I may consider to be my patron and protector' and he added tactfully 'I presume there is an order in the Treasury'.

This fragment of the report demonstrates just how difficult a position Nash was in, attempting to serve two masters, but at no time allowing the situation to undermine his loyalty to the Sovereign. The development of Carlton House Gardens led to the adjacent development of St James Park for which the Treasury gave orders in 15 January 1827. Nash designed three long terraces along the north side of the park and three of unequal length for the south side. Two only of the northern terraces were built, known today as Carlton Terrace east and west, the lodges that Nash proposed to be dotted about the Park were not constructed and his wide carriageway improvement to the Mall was not implemented as planned.

Nash dealt with the park layout in true Reptonian style, converting a large area of scrubland with a straight canal through the site, into a long sweeping lake with islands and planting the whole with trees and shrubs. Nash's gardener from East Cowes personally supervised the works. Other detail improvements proposed under Nash's plans were not approved by the 1828 Committee and although Nash was subjected to severe scrutiny and a degree of implied censure there was no suggestion that his integrity, or professional competence was anything but sound. The issue revolved around the seemingly loose and irresponsible control of public money.

The matter was again debated in the House during May 1829 when a personal attack on Nash was made in respect of improper land valuations and purchases at Suffolk Street and Regents Park. A motion was carried shortly after, on 27 May and a further select committee sat to take evidence, Nash was not called, but prepared a lengthy statement [1] in his defence. However, once again, the committee's findings completely exonerated Nash, but concluded that it would be advisable if official architects were prevented from interesting themselves in property, for which they might be called upon to give a valuation[2].

It would seem at this stage both public opinion and Nash's friends were reassured of his integrity. The King obviously felt a deep resentment that his *protégé* should have been so publicly persecuted without justification and was moved to write to the Prime Minister.

1 - Nash Statement 1829
2 - 1829 Report

Royal Lodge   *14 June 1829*

My Dear Friend,

I now write to you upon a matter in which I feel very much interested. The Report of the Committee of the House of Commons upon Mr Nash's business has been delivered in, and, as I am informed by one of that Committee (not one of those who had any previous predilection towards him) "without the slightest stain or imputation upon or against his character", I do therefore desire that you will direct his being gazetted by himself on Tuesday next, the 16th of this month, as a Baronet, with the remainder at his death (as he, Nash, has no family of his own), to his Nephew Mr Edwards, a gentleman of excellent character, large property, who sat in the last Parliament, and who has proved himself a thorough supporter of government, and a most loyal man, besides being well known to me personally. Mr Nash has been most infamously used, and there is but one opinion about it: and therefore it is not only an act of justice to him but to my own dignity, that this should forthwith be done. For if those who go through the furnace for me and for my service, are not protected, the favour of the Sovereign becomes worse than nugatory.

Your very sincere friend
G.R.

The Duke of Wellington was however not sympathetic to Nash's case and not prepared to agree to something of which he disapproved. His reply to the King was concise stating that the report of the select committee had not been before the House and that His Majesty 'would not wish to confer an honour upon an individual while his conduct is, or for as the public knows, still under enquiry'. Furthermore that the proper moment to confirm the honour was at the completion of Buckingham Palace which was to be Christmas next. So Nash's honour was not gazetted and Mr Nash he remained, but such was the esteem that he was held in by the King that an honour of this level was intended.

One year after the exchange of letters the King died, peacefully at Windsor. He was not to see his palace completed and by this time circumstances were completely out of control. The Government was then able to make uninhibited enquiries into the financial excess of the whole project and consequently Nash's career ended forthwith. During October 1830 The Treasury suspended his commission at the Board of Works and all work at the Palace ceased. Yet another select committee was formed, to examine in detail, Nash's methods of estimating and contracting and as from March 3 1831 severe cross examinations commenced. As ever, James Pennethorne, Nash's chief assistant and supervisor of many of the metropolitan improvements was there to give what support he could to his master. It was claimed that Nash had sold bricks[1] from his own kilns at Norwood to palace contractors to his advantage and that it was necessary to review his working relationships with tradesmen, but after long and tedious examinations nothing out of order was found.

Nash's contemporaries, the other attached architects, were called as was the Assistant Surveyor General to report on the structural condition of the building and to examine the costs of the outstanding works through to completion. Four months later a report was presented and Nash was subjected to the humiliating criticisms of those who previously had to respect him as the foremost architect. Two engineers and an iron-founder were called, who attempted to establish that Nash's construction was unsound, because of his use of iron support members. This was not proven and site examinations indicated no sign of weakness or deflection. The way in which the contract for this material was placed and Nash's empirical manner of structural design was, however, criticised.

Nash wrote to the committee expressing his disgust at the nature of the proceedings and concluded that:-

'The Building is in every part perfectly secure; and I call upon them to make any fair or just experiments they may think proper to justify the opinions they have given; at present every part of their Report is founded on conjecture, on opinions merely ASSERTED, not proved; or where attempted to be founded on facts, the facts STATED are NOT BORNE OUT'.

Not withstanding any credibility restored, from the committee's findings, Nash was finished, nobody in authority was prepared consider retaining his services, he had failed through his seemingly total disregard of financial control.

This point was consolidated in the committee's official findings[2] laid before Parliament on 14 October 1831 and Nash was censured for the gross inaccuracies of his estimate of May 1829 and for the irregular contractual arrangements. The committee concurred with the criticisms detailed in the Treasury minute of 15 October 1830, other than any evidence of Nash having wilfully concealed the excesses of the estimate from the Treasury. Whilst Nash was charged with inexcusable irregularity and great negligence, the view was taken that successive governments had not substantiated the content of estimates brought before Parliament. Any threat of personal prosecution against him as a consequence diminished.

---

1 - *Nash's bricks were of uneven form and only suitable for the construction of thick walls. Larger than normal 10½ inches in length, rose 13 inches in four courses as compared with the standards 12 inches. Each brick was marked with an N*

2 - *1831 Report*

1793 - 1835 : The Nash Epoch

The unfinished Palace was a subject of derision and suggestions for its use were fair game for critics of the time. Nevertheless the committee reported that the architect Edward Blore, not previously associated with royal works, had been approached to evaluate the cost of work required to complete the Palace for the new Sovereign William IV and his consort. A figure of £75,000 was agreed by the Treasury and in November 1830 the completion of Nash's work authorised and entrusted to Blore. The cost of converting Buckingham House into Buckingham Palace originally estimated at a figure not less than £200,000 had at that stage cost £613,269 and by completion exceeded the 1825 estimate by a factor of almost 3.5. The completion involved various modifications, the removal of the dome, and the box tops from the pavilions, filling the voids created between the centre part of the garden front and the north and south pavilions and finally raising the height of the wings by the addition of a continuous attic.

In so doing diminishing still further what picturesque qualities Nash's design had originally possessed.

iv Island Retreat

On 26 October 1830 Nash acknowledged the Treasury's dismissal with 'very great surprise and sorrow' and in February of the following year despatched a long but unconvincing letter in defence of his conduct and extenuating circumstances. Nash, however, must have been philosophical, realising that the situation at the Palace had become an uncontrollable nightmare, from which there would be an ultimate punitive awakening. The apportionment of blame had left his professional reputation all but intact, but he had become isolated, having lost his long standing ally and bulwark against the abusive prosaics of the time. Nash had been toppled from the highest position of power accomplished by an architect, toward the low estate so ironically and fatalistically related to Joseph Farington in 1821.

There is one other event to recall that must have encouraged Nash to take stock and consider the wider implications of his circumstances. During January 1830, Sir Thomas Lawrence, President of the Royal Academy and the most acclaimed portrait painter of the day, died. Nash had sat for him between 1825 and 1827 for a portrait commissioned by Jesus College, Oxford in recognition of Nash's help in negotiations over College property at the southern end of the new London Bridge. The portrait was exhibited at the Royal Academy during 1827.

Lawrence was buried at St.Paul's on 21 January and Nash was among the great assembly in the ice cold cathedral. Soon afterwards he became ill suffering the effect of some kind of stroke, described by Nash some months later, as 'a sudden rush of blood to the head, occasioned as the physicians say, by standing on the marble pavement in St Paul's Cathedral --- the effect of which was, at first privation of sight, and ever since, pain and giddiness in the head'. From this illness Nash was never to completely recover.

For the greater part of 1830 Nash was probably convalescing at East Cowes whilst his chief assistant Pennethorne and his managing clerk, Browne, ran the office and supervised the vast ornamental works at the Palace. During April of that year a letter was sent to Nash from John Stewart, Assistant Secretary at the treasury, soliciting an explanation of the expenditure in excess of the final estimate given by him to the Chancellor in May 1829. At what date the letter actually reached Nash is not known, but is seems inexplicable that for nearly six months it remained unanswered. Presumably Pennethorne and Browne were ignorant of the Palace accounts and not able to respond on Nash's behalf, alternatively Nash may have felt that the issue could be resolved after completion, given the 'Royal' interest in the specifications.

This must have also been a time for reflection,the hope and craving for the honour, postponed by Wellington, the prospect of his last few years as 'Sir John' and the founder of a titled family. So much so, that when Nash learned that the King's condition was critical he wrote to his friend and Royal secretary, William Knighton in an attempt to extract from the dying Monarch a definitive bestowal of the intended Baronetcy. The letter, most uncharacteristically Nash, was crudely formed and full of embarrassment and servility, was to no avail, there was no edit from the royal death bed.

By August 1830, just a few weeks after the King's death, Nash's health had improved to an extent that he was reported to have been seen in the grounds of the Pavilion [1] with William IV, perhaps making a final attempt to re-establish his royal patronage or explain the complicated detail of the Palace affairs. During September he was again, deeply embroiled in the estimates and finally replied to the Treasury on 29 September, totally unable to reconcile the ascertained expenditure against the estimates.

Following the humiliating experience of his eventual dismissal, Nash spent most of his time at East Cowes, returning to London and elsewhere to fulfil social and business engagements. Pennethorne was left in charge of Regent Street and the only metropolitan work of note to occupy Nash, was the design of the National Gallery on the north side of the newly formed Charing Cross, a commission ultimately awarded to Wilkins.

At East Cowes, Nash presented a design for a simple Gothic church, across the Park from the castle. A neighbour donated the site and on 6 September 1831 Princess Victoria, assisted by her mother the Duchess of Kent, laid the foundation stone in the tower of the new church. This, the first public engagement of a girl of twelve, who during her life time was to lay many more foundation stones and as Queen Victoria, six years later, was the first sovereign to hold Court in Buckingham Palace.

The surviving Nash diary for 1832 gives a fascinating insight to the very full life the architect continued to lead despite his enforced semi-retirement and slowly deteriorating health. Nash had settled into a routine of social gatherings, business commitments and the odd public engagement. There were long discussions with Browne and Nixon, who would seem to have been Nash's personal manager or agent, concerning the Palace accounts and there were days spent at the drawing board and the writing of reports. Nash's considerable design talents were still in demand and his social standing was in no way diminished by the events of 1831.

East Cowes Castle was a hospitable open house and hardly a day passed without visitors and dinner parties, both for casual callers and invited guests and other than some Sundays, the Nashes never dined alone. Virtually all the Island gentry visited on a regular basis as well as his neighbours, former clients and the clergy. James Pennethorne was held in special regard by Nash, he was the only person usually referred to simply by christian name, almost it would seem a son to Nash and as a consequence a regular visitor.

For a man of 80 years Nash was extremely active. During the summer months he would regularly walk to Whippingham Church on Sundays and return later in the day for a second service, a total of about eight miles. He frequently walked the grounds of his own estate, that of Norris, to East and West Cowes and to Northwood.

His diary records the following events for 1832 of random interest.

January and February are spent at East Cowes, March April and May in London and the Nashes return to East Cowes for the remainder of the year.

Monday 6 January	*Cowes. Went to Newport - Mr Hewett, Mr Eastwick and Mifs Chapman dined with us - Fanny Ward came to stay a few days*
Thursday 12 January	*Cowes. Walked 5 miles in Conservatory Emma & Charlotte Ward & Mr & Mrs Hewett & Col William Hewett dined with us - Mr Eastwick came in the evening.*

---

1 - *Brighton Herald 21 August 1830.*

East Cowes Castle

Thursday 17 January	*Cowes - Went to Newport to make affidavit to receive my annuity - Mifs Goodrich dined with us*
Thursday 19 January	*Cowes - better - Walked two miles and a half before break fast - Went to Newport to sign certificate for annuity having done it wrong the other day* (proving Nash was only human after all)
Saturday 21 January	*Cowes - Went over to West Cowes to see Lord Belfasts new building - went afterwards to inspect the repairs at Norris* (It would seem Nash was supervising repairs at Norris Castle for Lord George Seymour)
Friday 3 February	*Cowes - drawing all day for the garden in the Regents Park*
Thursday 9 February	*Cowes - Went to Hamstead to meet the Committee of the Shalfleet Vestry came home to dinner*
Thursday 14 February	*Cowes - Sent Lord Belfast his plans - Mr & Mrs Hewitt & Mrs Wm Hewett - Mifs Barton, George, Richard & Fanny Ward dined with us*
Wednesday 22 February	*Cowes - Church Committee held a meeting here to consider the con tracts for the roof - Emma & Charlotte Ward dined with us* (This is the roof for St James Church)
Wednesday 29 February	*Left Cowes by the Emerald Steamer, landed at Southampton at 1/2 past 7 slept there.*
Friday 2 March	*London - Called at the office of Woods & Walked round to look at several of the new buildings - we dined at Mrs Vaughans*
Monday 12 March	*London - drove up to the Regents Park & the Village with Mrs Nash - we dined with Mrs Fitzroy*
Wednesday 28 March	*London - Lord Grey & Lord Duncannon called to see model for National Gallery - went in evening to hear a lecture on astronomy the Opera House*
Saturday 7 April	*London - drove round the Park with Mrs Nash & Mrs Parker, Emma & Charlotte Ward & the Mifs Villiers dined with us - Nixon came from Cowes. Walked to Marlborough Street.* (The Ward family also had a house in London)
Saturday 14 April	*London - met Lord Duncannon of Carlton House Stables - dined at Mr Delafields*
Sunday 22 April	*London - Walked to the Chapel Royal in the morning to Church & around St James Park in the afternoon with Mrs Parker. Maria Parker dined with us*

Tuesday 15 May

London - Not out - the Vaughans, Lyons, Hopkinsons & Mifs Tierney dined with - Lord Grey & his colleagues sent for by the King -The Duke of Wellington having failed to make a parliament
(Nash comments on the political affairs of the day)

Thursday 24 May

London - Mr Estwick, Nash Vaughans & Mrs Bloomfield dined with us - went to Mrs Vaughans Ball - stayed till past 3

Friday 1 June

Left Fareham & drove down to Portsmouth crossed by the 3 o'clock steamer - the carriage & horses did the same to Ryde

Sunday 3 June

Cowes - Walked to Whippingham Church - Mr Hoffins did the duty - Fanny Ward dined with us

Tuesday 12 June

At the Farms all the morning walking about - caught in a thunder storm - returned to Cowes after dinner arrived there about 8 to tea

Friday 15 June

Cowes - Mrs Parker came by the morning Steamer & returned in the afternoon - after dinner drove to Heathfield and back - wrote to James
(Nash's other farm at Heathfield)

Saturday 16 June

Cowes - Walked to East Cowes to see the launch of a Brig built for Ld Belfast
After dinner drove to Newport.
(Nash attends the launch of the 'Waterwich' 331 Tons)

Sunday 17 June

Cowes - Walked to Whippingham to Church Lord & Lady G. Seymour - Lord & Lady Boyle the Wards & Mifs Goodrich came to tea

Thursday 28 June

Cowes - Walked with Mr Duncan to see the new Church before breakfast & to see him on board the steamer afterwards. He left us - Sir George Thomas dined with us & Lord George Seymour came to tea.

Thursday 12 July

Cowes - Went to Gatcombe with Mrs Nash & Mrs Vaughan to call upon Col Campbell

Tuesday 24 July

Cowes Mr & Mrs Walter Hook left us by afternoon steamer. Went down with them to E.Cowes - Mr & Mrs Lyon & children came

Monday 6 August

Cowes - Mr & Mrs Lyon left us by the 11 o'clock Steamer - Mr Hook came - the Seymours & Blachfords & Mr B Lyon dined with us - Nixon arrived from Town.

Tuesday 14 August

Cowes - busy all day with letters Mr Stewart of Killymoon Clerk of the Works about repairing his house - The Seymours dined with us.

Thursday 16 August

Cowes - Went to an archery party at Lady Holmes with the Carletons & Lyons.

East Cowes Castle

Thursday 23 August	*Cowes - Drove to Carisbrooke to settle with the Stewards the arrangements for the archery - Henry Litolff a first rate pianist dined and slept with us & we had a large soiree*
	(Nash is host to the pianist and his father at East Cowes just days after his first public performance at Covent Garden Theatre on July 24 1832. Litolff was a child prodigy of fourteen at this time.)
Wednesday 5 September	*Cowes. Went to the Needles, Alum Bay & Freshwater - dined there. Came home to tea the Villiers & Listers made our party and went with us.*
Thursday 13 September	*Cowes - Wet morning - the Bishop of Rochester called - the Carletons came to dine & sleep - The Seymours & Lord George, Mr Ward, Mr Lathorne & Mr White dined with us.*
Friday 21 September	*Cowes - Went to the back of the Island to call upon Mrs Copley. Took a luncheon dinner with her - called at Sir W.Gooding & Mrs Vine - drank tea at the Sandrock Hotel. Got home at 1/2 past 9.*
Wednesday 26 September	*Hamstead Farm - Walked to the rail road afterwards with Mrs Nash down to the sea - dined at 4 - Wheeler the Clerk of Shalfleet Parish called - talked to him about the poor.*
Friday 12 October	*Cowes - attended a vestry meeting at Whippingham Church to consider of the support and employment of the Poor. Captn Beckford & Mr Saunders called.*
Thursday 25 October	*Cowes - busy at accounts - Sir George Seymour called & the Wards & Mrs James, the Beckfords - Mr Atkinson, Mr Davids & the Smiths of Padmore dined with us.*
Monday 3 December	*Cowes - Parliament was dissolved this day.*
Thursday 20 December	*Cowes - Went over to West Cowes & voted for Sir Richd Simeon, he had a great majority. Mr Campbell resigned.*
Tuesday 25 December	*Cowes. James Pennethorne & Mr Turner came - went to Whippingham Church - stayed the Sacrament*
	(Nash spends Christmas with James Pennethorne & JMW Turner)

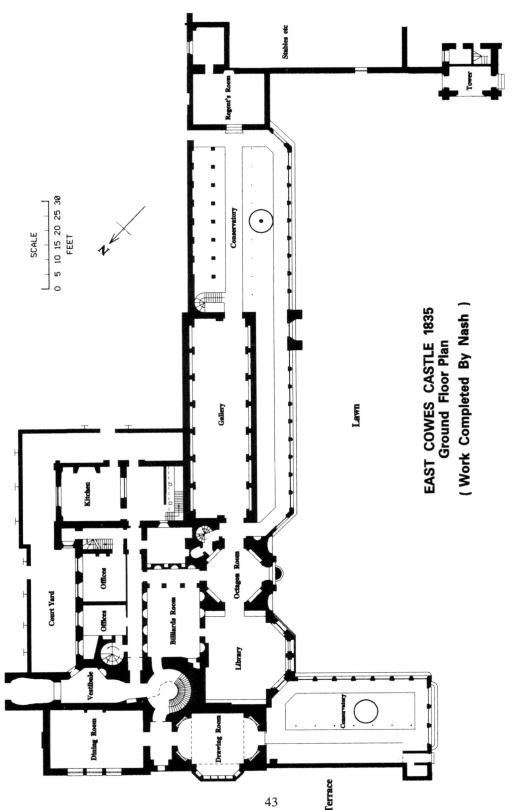

SCALE

0 5 10 15 20 25 30
FEET

N

Stables etc

Regent's Room

Tower

Conservatory

Gallery

Lawn

Kitchen

Court Yard

Offices

Offices

Billiards Room

Octagon Room

Library

Vestibule

Dining Room

Drawing Room

Conservatory

Terrace

EAST COWES CASTLE 1835
Ground Floor Plan
(Work Completed By Nash)

FIGURE 9

By way of contrast James Pennethorne's diary for the same year indicates a gradual taking over of the remaining business interests of the practice. Numerous meetings regarding Carlton House Terrace, with Blore regarding the Palace, the Ophthalmia building in Albany Street and the Park Villages. It is Pennethorne who provides the designs for an important commission[1] for the Ward family at West Cowes. There are visits to East Cowes to see Nash, travelling by the night mail coach to Southampton and arriving on the Island at breakfast time.

Christmas 1832 was spent at East Cowes after travelling down from London on the 'Eclipse' coach arriving at Southampton at 7.30 and staying overnight at the Coach & Horses. Meeting Turner[2] the following morning and experiencing a rough crossing to Cowes by steam and staying the remaining part of the week at the castle. On New Years eve Mr G Ward [3], the prospective parliamentary candidate was present at the castle for dinner.

Nash's diary for the years 1833 and 1834 do not survive, but during 1833 Nash was much saddened by the sudden death, during August, of his only relative John Edwards, at the age of sixty-one. He died at his Regent Street house and this finally encouraged Nash to leave London for good. His renowned art gallery at 14 Regent Street was stripped in its entirety, shipped to the Island and reassembled in the north-eastern corner of the long conservatory at East Cowes.
(figure 9)

In the Spring of 1834 he finally wrote to Alexander Milne at the Office of Woods:-

---

East Cowes Castle
March 22nd 1834

My dear Sir,

I have quitted London and resigned my Professional practice to Mr Pennethorne. I have deposited with him all my Papers, Plans and Designs of every kind relative to the Regents Park, New Street, Saint James's Park, Carlton House Terrace, and Buckingham House, and other matters connected with your office in order that the Commissioners may have access to them, he being, as you know, as perfectly acquainted with every detail as I am myself, and in communicating this circumstance to your Board I beg most gratefully to thank them for every favour and indulgence which they have for so many years shown me, and I earnestly recommend Mr Pennethorne to their patronage, as perhaps the last act of kindness they can do me, and being well assured that he will acquit himself in all respects to my hope and to their satisfaction - and to say that if at any time my co-operation can be of use to their Board it will be most grateful to me to render it.

I have the honour to be, My dear Sir,
Your faithful Servant
John Nash.

---

1 - *Probably an extension to Northwood House or the Gothic Villa known as Moor House.*
2 - *J.M.W.Turner who had been visiting Petworth.*
3 - *Mr G.H.Ward.*

Attached was a long list of plans, drawings and other documents relating to the London practice.

Nash's retirement from there on should have been unimpaired, but for some years there had been speculation about the level of his debts. As early as 1821 Westall[1], the painter, had told Farington that information from 'three different quarters' had Nash 'at a stand in money matters' owing £800,000 if not £1,000,000. This would have been during his heavy speculation in the Quadrant and the Regent's Canal schemes and may have been a 'snapshot' balance, but in any case he was still able to spend money freely on the castle, Hamstead and his house in Regent Street. A debt of £800 at this time to the Canal Company which Nash found 'inconvenient' to repay places the issue in its proper perspective.

However, at the beginning of 1833 Nash was in debt to the value of around £16,000 to a banking Company of Lombard Street[2]. He had arranged repayment over a long period through John Robert Ward, son of his old friend and business associate George Ward, John Ward was a partner in the banking Company. He met with financial disaster in 1833 and as a consequence Nash was pressed for the outstanding amount, and was forced to sell real estate in a falling market at a fraction of its true value. Nevertheless by July 1834 Nash had repaid the capital and interest charges apart from around £500 which was secured against title deeds lodged with the Bank.

There followed a further call from an unexpected quarter that placed additional pressure on Nash's already stretched finances for the amount of £3,000. This he was not able to meet because of the fraudulent act of a person whom Nash had regarded as a friend and in whom he had placed great trust[3]. The result being that in 1834 Nash was extremely short of money, his stated reason being ' my capital was embarked in Houses, and in materials for Building, both of which, at the present epoch, were most difficult to turn into cash.'

During October of that year Nash made a new Will, naming Mrs Nash, George Henry Ward and James Pennethorne as executors and leaving the whole of his estate to Mrs Nash. Attempting no doubt, to provide for her the maximum security whatever misfortunes might occur after his death.

The other surviving diary of 1835 provides a picture of an old man rapidly failing in health, no longer able to rise early and coming to terms with the imposed restrictions of his illness. He endures good and bad days but his mind is ever active and alert. His diary neat and precise as ever, records the details of his life up until two days before his death.

Thursday January 1 *Cowes - a middling night but not well in the day - not up till 1/2 past 11 came to bed at 10 - Mr Shedden called & Mr Phillip.*

Friday January 9 *Cowes - up at 9 - drove to Newport with Mrs Nash & Sophie Parker - called at Mr Wards committee at the Bank & at Mr Sewells*

Sunday January 11 *Cowes. a pretty good night - down to breakfast at 10 - Mrs Nash ill all day. Sir George Seymour drank Tea with us.*

1 - *William Westall a noted artist and engraver produced several views of the Isle of Wight between the years 1836 - 1842*
2 - *Vere, Sapt, Banbury and Co., formerly Vere, Ward & Co.*
3 - *Summerson 1980 (C13, P186)*

Monday January 26

Cowes - Sent all the late Mr John Ward's letters to Nixon - Gen¹ Mainwaring called Lady Mary Arnold & Charlotte Ward up at 9 came to bed a little before 10.

Friday February 6

Cowes - Dictated letter to Bernasconi, got up very well and had a good day Emma & Nora Ward called (Bernasconi was a plaster worker used by Nash at Carlton Terrace)

Thursday February 19

Cowes - not up till eleven - the Archdeacon Hill called - dictated short letter to Nixon - signed two agreements for letting part of Ophthalmia.

Sunday March 1

Cowes - Mr Smith dined with us at 8 o'clock. Mr Baugh the new curate dined & slept.
(Mr Baugh is the new Curate at St James)

Sunday March 8

Cowes - Mr Ward called & Lord Yarborough

Friday March 13

Cowes - Nixon came and returned to Town by the nights mail talking over building with him - Mr & Mrs Hewett & 2 of their children came to dine with us.

Monday March 16

Cowes - Sir Henry Thompson & Mr Oglander called - not up till near 12.

Saturday March 21

Cowes - Not up till near 11 - walked along the conservatory to the room at the end.

Saturday April 4

Cowes - not up till past 2 - rather middling - heard from Nixon signed letter to Mr Lyon to authorise him to cancel Nixon's lease of the brick yard.

Saturday April 11

Cowes - not up till near 2 - not so well as yesterday - felt weary sick at dinner & ate nothing.

Sunday April 19

Cowes - got up at 11, not down stairs all day - Mr Ward & Mr Baugh dined here. (Easter day 1835 Nash confined to his bed).

Thursday April 30

Cowes - Sat up while they made the bed much the same as yesterday.

Saturday May 2

Cowes - Saw Mr Lyon and shook hands with him - sat up at night to have the bed made.
(Nash sees his Solicitor for the last time his gesture perhaps indicating his acceptance of the inevitable).

Monday May 4

Cowes - Took a little castor oil in the morning - sat up in the evening to have the bed made & be shaved.

Tuesday May 5

Cowes - not able to get out of bed without assistance. Sleeping all day, Mrs Nash ill.

Wednesday May 6	*Cowes - very ill indeed all day.*
Sunday May 10	*Cowes - very ill.*
Monday May 11	*Cowes - much worse.*
	(Nash's last diary entry)

John Nash died at East Cowes on 13 May 1835.

His burial was held on 20 May at the little church of St James designed by Nash four years earlier. The coffin, legend records, was secreted down from the castle the night before to deny local creditors the opportunity of making the disagreeable gesture of arresting the corpse. A conventional monument, in the form of a sarcophagus, with simple *antefixa*, may not have been erected until the remains of Mrs Nash were laid with her husband in 1851.

The inscription records:

> **SACRED** to the Memory of
> **JOHN NASH** *ESQ.re.*
> of East Cowes Castle:
> *who departed this life*
> May 13th, 1835
> *Aged 83 years*
> ALSO, of **MARY ANN** *his wife*
> who died Febry 7th 1851
> *Aged 78 years.*
> **JOHN NASH**
> **ARCHITECT**

The word ARCHITECT was not inscribed until the 1970's, there previously being no acknowledgement of the once famous man's profession. At the time of his death sympathetic tributes were rare, Nash had disappeared from public view under a cloud of Parliamentary censure. The *Annual Register* simply recorded the popular view that 'As a speculative builder this gentleman amassed a large fortune; but as an architect he did not achieve anything that will confer upon him a lasting reputation'.

Just one editorial, in the *John Bull* of satirical fame, considered Nash's passing worthy of sensitive tribute. Its writer, Theodore Hook, had known Nash for some years, both in London and East Cowes and his brother as Rector of Whippingham had been the local parson.

His article, in defence of the architect expressed that Nash; 'was the loyal servant of a kind and generous master whom he never betrayed by justifying himself at his master's expense. Criticism of the structural stability of the palace had proved completely unfounded as the indictments of the architect's professional integrity in other circumstances. His architecture might or might not be wholly admirable - that was a matter of taste. But on what he had done for London there could be no two opinions:

Let the readers recollect the huddled mass of wretched streets and houses which twenty years ago covered the site of Regent Street, the Quadrant and Waterloo Place; let the reader recollect the still more wretched courts and alleys, dens of infamy and haunts of thieves, which maze-like spread themselves from St.Martin's Church to the neighbourhood of Covent Garden; let him now look upon the range of buildings and the handsome streets which occupy their places .... Let the reader, we say turn his eyes to the magnificent adjunct of London, the Regent's Park, now one of the healthiest and gayest of the public walks and drives, a creation of the mind of Mr Nash. Look at the manner in which the interior of St.James's Park was in a few months converted from a swampy meadow into a luxurious garden, and then, let the reader ask himself whether the metropolis is or is not indebted to the taste and genius of the much traduced object of this notice.'

Then Hook spoke of Nash himself:

'In private life Mr Nash was a warm and sincere friend, his mind active and comprehensive as it was, was singularly natural and simple; his thoughts were original, and his conversation was both instructive and pre-eminently agreeable. He was in fact, a most extraordinary man.'

The passage of time and the work of Nash's twentieth century biographers have enabled us to view his achievements in a more informed and balanced way. Because of Nash and through him great works were accomplished, the interaction with his royal patron created the climate and the acceptability. Men flourished under his leadership, their talents encouraged and not in any way curtailed, the likes of Pugin, Pennethorne and Burton were enriched by this association.

Today Nash is more widely appreciated than his contemporaries, if there is a criticism perhaps he lacked the focused concentration for detail. Nevertheless his vision, pursued inexorably, has conferred a range of extant buildings which serve to underline the achievement of the age.

Almost one hundred and sixty years after the death of John Nash a significant event has closed the chapter of the Nash epoch. During the summer of 1993 the doors of Buckingham Palace have been open for all to see the magnificent series of Classical interiors, originally designed by Nash and completed during those dark days of Parliamentary censure and public scandal.

Having taken the opportunity to view these treasures, locked away for so many years, I believe that we can safely leave the last word with Nash.

1. Downton Castle, Herefordshire : built by Richard Payne Knight in 1774. It was to inspire Nash's castle-house cycle.

2. The picturesque setting of Downton Castle : from an engraving by J.Powell after T.Herne c1801.

3. East Cowes Castle from the north-west : the initial concept. From an engraving featured in Cooke's New Picture of the Isle of Wight, published 1808.

4. Norris Castle 1799-1805 : reproduced from the original pencil and brown wash by Tom Pennethorne 1815.

5. East Cowes Castle entrance front : the front elevation of the castle as completed by Nash. A Brannon engraving commissioned privately by Nash 1826.

6. East Cowes Castle north-west front: as completed by Nash and much altered from the original elevation of 1802. A Brannon engraving commissioned privately by Nash 1826.

7. The dining-room at East Cowes Castle : a photograph taken during the early part of the century and described by Joseph Farington in 1817.

8. The drawing-room at East Cowes Castle : Nash's Paris Directoire drawing-room photographed during the early part of the century and described by Joseph Farington in 1817.

9. The library at East Cowes Castle : Nash's library and octagon room beyond, photographed during the early part of the century and described by Joseph Farington in 1817. The decorations have been somewhat enriched since that time and the coat of arms is not that of Nash

10. The long walk within the walled garden : Nash's fertile terraced garden of which he was very proud. Photographed in 1934.

11. The garden conservatories of East Cowes Castle : the modern replacement for Nash's original conservatories. Photographed during 1934

13. A garden statue : 'Bacchante by Golti' within the formal gardens at East Cowes Castle.

12. The ornamental garden fountain : situated within the formal garden at East Cowes Castle, photographed in 1884

14A/B. The development of the long conservatory at East Cowes Castle : the Brannon engravings of 1824 and 1831 indicate the development of Nash's long conservatory, believed to have been completed during 1824.

15. The conservatories at East Cowes Castle : Nash's tour de force, the claustral setting of conservatory arches. Photographed during the early part of the century.

16. East Cowes Castle distant view from the south-west : a Brannon engraving commissioned privately by Nash in 1827.

17. The conservatory entrance from the lawn : a photograph taken in 1884.

18. Buckingham Palace c1830 : completed to Nash's design with the triumphal Marble Arch as its centre piece.

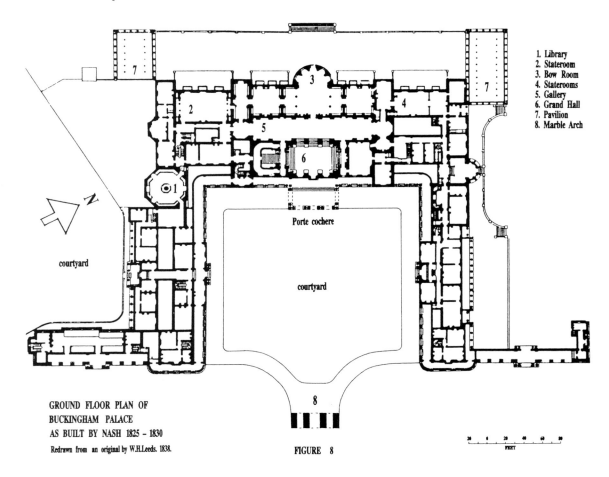

1. Library
2. Stateroom
3. Bow Room
4. Staterooms
5. Gallery
6. Grand Hall
7. Pavilion
8. Marble Arch

Porte cochere

courtyard

courtyard

GROUND FLOOR PLAN OF
BUCKINGHAM PALACE
AS BUILT BY NASH 1825 - 1830

Redrawn from an original by W.H.Leeds. 1838.

FIGURE 8

FEET

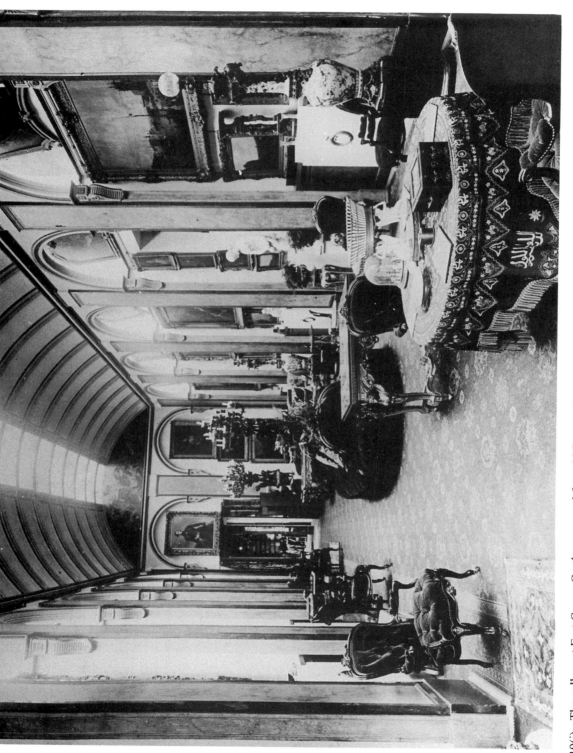

19(i). The gallery at East Cowes Castle : removed from 14 Regent Street during 1834 and re-erected within the long conservatory. A photograph taken during the early part of the century, looking towards the octagon room.

19(ii). The gallery at East Cowes Castle: a photograph taken during the early part of the century looking towards the long conservatory

	£ s d	£ s d	£ s d
Brought forward	" " "	" " "	6858 . 13 . 4½
East Cowes Castle Account	Year 1832	Year 1833	
Gardeners Wages	" " "	274 . 16 . 9	
Garden expences	" " "	55 . 9 . 2½	
Corn for Horses	" " "	2 . 12 . 8	
Dust's Salary & Board Wages	" " "	91 . 13 . "	
Tradesmens bills for Garden	22 . 9 . "	" " "	
do . . . . do . . for Shaw & Corn .	55 . 5 . 6	" " "	
Smith & Farriers Account	6 . 1 . 2	" " "	
Taxes Rates Tythes &c	1 . 16 . 8	82 . 9 . 9	
Tradesmens bills for House	93 . 6 . "	80 . 12 . 9	
Sundry Household expences	" " "	5 . 9 . 7	
Donation to James	" " "	6 . 10 . "	
Sheep purchased	" " "	58 . 19 . "	
Servants Board Wages	" " "	13 . 12 . "	
Building account per John Taylor . .	" " "	129 . 16 . "	
Tradesmens bills & expences for do . . .	" " "	31 . 15 . "	
	178 . 18 . 4		
		833 . 15 . 8½	
		1012 . 14 . 0½	
Deduct balance of Dust's acco.t unpaid . . .		18 . 14 . 1	
			993 . 19 . 11½
		£	7852 . 13 . 4

20(i). Nash's Business Accounts: typical entries from the ledger for the castle accounts,

$\mathcal{C}^r$

	£ . d	Year 1832 £ . d	Year 1833 £ . d	£ . d
Brought forw⁴				4203 . 3 . 11
Heathfield Farm Account		Year 1832	Year 1833	
		£ . d	£ . d	
Labourers Wages		" "	53 . 15 . 1	
Task Work		" "	3 . 6 . 8¾	
Women day work		" "	" 7 . 6	
Blacksmith		" "	" 1 . 3	
Threshers work		" "	3 . 7 . 1	
Poor rate		" "	4 "	
Highway rate		" "	1 . 2 . 1	
Purchase of 2 Cows & 1 Calf ...		" "	17 . 2 ..	
d⁰ .... of 1 Sow & 5 Pigs ...		" "	4 . 10 ..	
d⁰ .... of 1 Horse ...	9 " "			
Church rate	. 8 . 4			
Tradesmens bills	52 . 16 . 6		36 . 10 . 8	
Incidental expences			4 . 11	
Allowances to Gladdis			20 . 17 . 4	
	62 . 4 . 10		149 . 13 . 8¾	
			62 . 4 . 10	
			211 . 18 . 6¾	
By Cash paid to Sir R⁴ Bassell &C⁰ to 10ᵗᵐ				
Nixon's a/c			39 . 1 . 3	251 " 10
Hamstead Farm				
Improvement Account		year 1832	Year 1833	
New Plantation Account		" " "	45 . 12 . 7½	
Nursery d⁰ ... d⁰		" " "	14 . 5 . 3	
Old Plantation d⁰		" " "	1 . 5	
Road making & repairing		" " "	42 . 10 . 10	
Draining Arable land		" " "	88 . 5 . 7½	
Purchase of Dung		" " "	153 . 7 . 6	
Freightage of d⁰		" " "	14 . 5 .	
Unloading Dung		" " "	3 . 12 . 6	
Rail road	165 . 19 . 6		183 . 12 . " 4	
Ornamental water	409 . 1 . 6½		3 . 12 . 10	
Building to Farm house	45 . 16 . 8		413 . 1 . 6¼	
Rail road Avenues		" " "	3 . 2 . 7½	
Stock account	72 . 6 . 7		" " "	
Incidental expences		" " "	52 . 10 . 8½	
Renewing & Planting Belts in Plantation ..		" " "	196 . 3 . 6	
Repairs of the Sloop Wellington ...	5 . 9 . 3½		" 5 "	
Ross on acc⁴ of Salary		" " "	75 . 2 . 6	
Charles Nixon Salary		" " "	15 . "	
Wilkinson on acc⁴ of purchase of Tythe ...		" " "	400 " "	
		698 . 13 . 7		
			1705 . 15 . 0½	2404 . 8 . 7¾
Carried forward			£	6858 . 13 . 4½

20(ii) Hamstead and Heathfield Farm

21. North Lodge : Nash's rustic cottage marking the entrance to East Cowes Castle. From a
    Brannon engraving of 1820.

22. Sandrock Hotel Niton : one of Nash's favourite haunts in the south of the Isle of Wight.
    From a Barber engraving c1834.

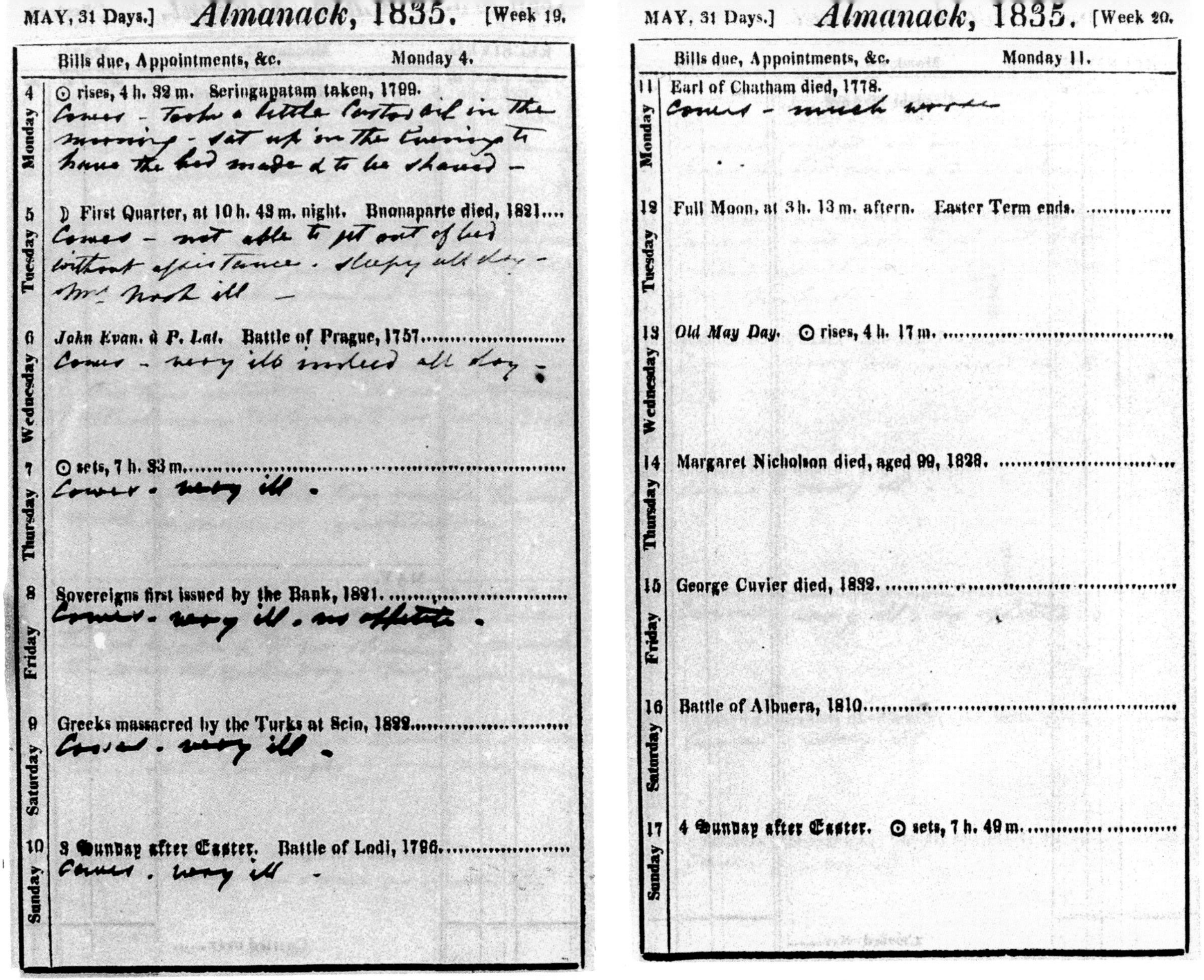

MAY, 31 Days.]   *Almanack, 1835.*   [Week 19.

Monday 4.

	Bills due, Appointments, &c.
4 Monday	☉ rises, 4 h. 32 m. Seringapatam taken, 1799. *Corner – Tooke a little better, at in the morning; but not in the evening to know the bed mode it to be chance) –*
5 Tuesday	
6 Wednesday	☽ First Quarter, at 10 h. 49 m. night. Buonaparte died, 1821. *Corner – not able to get out of bed without assistance. Sleepy all day – Mrs. Nash ill –*
7 Thursday	John Evan. & P. Lat. Battle of Prague, 1757. *Corner – very ill: involved all day :*
8 Friday	☉ sets, 7 h. 33 m. *Corner – very ill –*
9 Saturday	Sovereigns first issued by the Bank, 1821. *Corner – very ill. Leave – .... very ill – ....*
10 Sunday	Greeks massacred by the Turks at Scio, 1822. *Mr. Nash – very ....*
	3 Sunday after Easter. Battle of Lodi, 1796. *Corner – very ill –*

MAY, 31 Days.]   *Almanack, 1835.*   [Week 20.

Monday 11.

	Bills due, Appointments, &c.
11 Monday	Earl of Chatham died, 1778. Easter Term ends. *Corner – ....*
12 Tuesday	Full Moon, at 3 h. 13 m. aftern.
13 Wednesday	Old May Day. ☉ rises, 4 h. 17 m.
14 Thursday	Margaret Nicholson died, aged 99, 1828.
15 Friday	George Cuvier died, 1832.
16 Saturday	Battle of Albuera, 1810.
17 Sunday	4 Sunday after Easter. ☉ sets, 7 h. 49 m.

23. Nash's
diary 1835 :
the final
entries in
John Nash's
diary written
at
East Cowes
Castle May
1835

The inscription on the sarcophagus reads:

SACRED to the Memory of
JOHN NASH Esqre
of East Cowes Castle
who departed this Life
May 13th 1835.
Aged 83 Years.
ALSO of MARY ANN his Wife
who died Feby 7th 1851.
Aged 78 Years.

JOHN NASH.
ARCHITECT

24. The Nash Sarcophagus : the plain sarcophagus of John and Mary Anne Nash at St. James's Church East Cowes

2

SHANNON TO GORT: 1835 - 1933

Because of pressing demands of the estate it was necessary for the executors named in Nash's Will to respond quickly. Such that the pictures from the castle, which included three works by Turner, two by West and copies of old masters painted by Richard Evans, were auctioned at Christie and Manson on 11 July 1835 and sold for a figure of £1,061[1]. The collection of books, medals and engravings were sold by Evans the bookseller on 15 July and realised £1,423[2]. The East Cowes Castle Estate was put up for sale and sold within the year to the Earl of Shannon, whose heir had recently married the daughter of Sir George Seymour, Nash's neighbour at Norris, for a disclosed figure of £20,000.

The total claims against Nash's estate were not recorded. However by 1841 the debts had been settled in full and the following appeared in one of the more light hearted columns of *The Times* on 29 December of that year:

> **BETTER LATE THAN NEVER. The executors of Mr John Nash the Architect of Regent Street, who died on 13th May 1835, at his castle in the Isle of Wight, have given notice of their being in a situation to pay his debts in full. We believe they amount to £15,000. Not bad Christmas news for those interested.**

Nash's Hamstead property was not sold and following the sale of the castle, Mrs Nash and Ann Pennethorne took up residence at the Manor and lived there for the rest of their lives.

The Earl of Shannon lived at East Cowes for some years and during this time the castle was also known as Shannon Castle. The house and grounds were at times open to the general public to view, but restricted when the family were in residence, this fact signified by the hoisting of a flag from the octagon tower flag staff.

Barber's *Picturesque Illustrations of the Isle of Wight* published in 1845 included a print of the castle[3], denoted 'The Seat of the Earl of Shannon' and displaying the Earl's crest. The print similar to the issue ten years earlier described as 'The Seat of John Nash Esq.' Barber's impressions of East Cowes and Norris Castle at this time are most interesting and merit comparison.

---

1 - Summerson 1980 P207 (40)
2 - A priced catalogue in the Soane Museum.
3 - Barbers print dated 1845, however, records indicate the property was occupied by Nathanial Burwell from 1843

East Cowes Castle

East Cowes Castle, now the property of the Earl of Shannon, stands on the brow of the hill that looks towards West Cowes, and, together with its grounds, forms a point of attraction with most visitors to either of those places. The site is well selected for a residence of the Gothic character; and the general effect of this castle, with its surrounding woods, must be admitted to be imposing. On a nearer inspection, it is seen to unite the features of the castellated mansion of a late date, with those of the baronial strong-hold of a much earlier period; the former, doubtless, for convenience, the latter for the sake of antiquated and striking appearance. Whether such an union be consistent with correct taste, is a question which perhaps may not improperly arise in the mind of the observer: in this, as in many other instances, we confess to have been but little struck with the propriety of machicolated towers frowning over the elegancies of domestic architecture. When time has divested a style of building of its objects and meaning, it should be either wholly laid aside, or, if adopted in the way of imitation, the imitation should be complete, and should admit of nothing incongruous: an axiom of this, which was but little studied by the late architect and proprietor of East Cowes Castle.

Norris Castle, a most conspicuous feature in the coast-view of this part of the Island, may be approached either by the road we have just quitted, or by a walk along the shore: the latter, of course, should be adopted only when the tide is favourable. Sir J.Wyattville (then Mr Wyatt) erected this singular structure for the late Lord Henry Seymour, who took much pride in it, and evidently received pleasure from the visits of strangers to his domain. As a specimen of the defensive architecture of the age which it affects, it certainly offers fewer incongruities that East Cowes Castle; yet, as a whole, it is infinitely less pleasing to the eye, as well as less elegant, than that edifice. The deception as to it's apparent antiquity, however, is complete to those unacquainted with the details of an ancient English castle; and numbers, who might first see Norris from the deck of a steam-boat, would be readily impressed with the idea that centuries had elapsed since the period of its erection. The grounds attached are open to the inspection of the public, and will repay the exertion of a stroll through them. The Stables, which are on a princely scale, the Pier, Bathing-House, and Sea-Walls, all erections of the late noble owner, merit at least passing attention from the visit.

There was a grandiose scheme devised during the period that Lord Shannon was resident at East Cowes Castle, that was to reshape the countryside to the south of the castle estate. In 1840 there were proposals to redevelop the ancient estate of East Shamblers into East Cowes Park. This consisted of a Botanical Garden surrounded by some 129 prestigious villas on large plots and a new road system including, ultimately, a new high road to the south of the Castle. However, by 1859 just 20 such villas had been constructed and by 1874 the proposals had been abandoned in favour of less grand residential development, more suited to the expanding industrial and commercial needs of the community. Significantly the new high road, initially private and the Villas bordering the castle estate were completed.

Following the ownership by the Earl of Shannon, sometime after 1841 and before 1854 when George Tudor purchased the Castle, there are two recorded owners. In 1843 Nathanial Burwell[1] and 1850 Charles Sawyer.

During the 1850's the Third Viscount Gort drifting towards bankruptcy, sold his estate in Ireland and in 1861 at the age of seventy-one, married the rich widow, Mrs Tudor the owner of East Cowes Castle. It was the second Viscount Gort, Charles Vereker, who in 1815 had so admired Nash's castle at East Cowes that he commissioned him to design a similar house at Lough Cutra, County Galway. There is an amusing story of the elderly Viscount's utmost surprise, when his new wife first introduced him to what was a vivid semblance of his old home.

1 - The tythe map of 1843 indicates the estate area of East Cowes Castle to be 45 acres

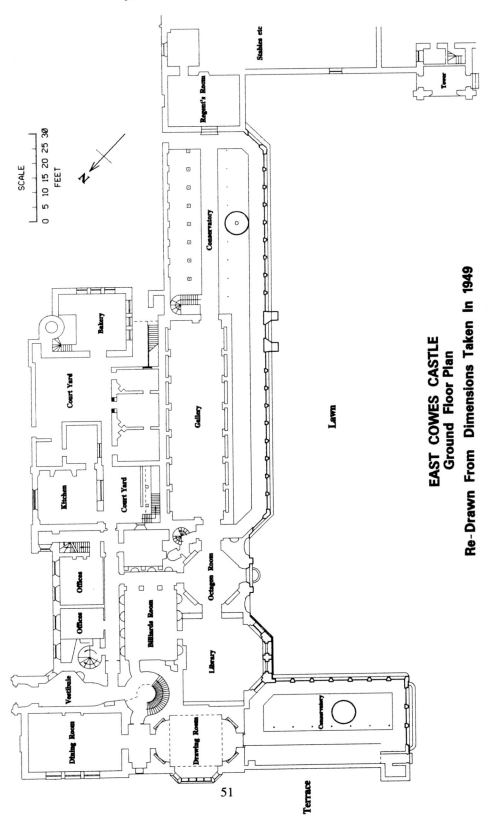

SCALE

0 5 10 15 20 25 30

FEET

Stables etc

Tower

Regent's Room

Conservatory

Bakery

Court Yard

Gallery

Kitchen

Court Yard

Lawn

Octagon Room

Offices

Offices

Billiards Room

Library

Vestibule

Conservatory

Dining Room

Drawing Room

Terrace

EAST COWES CASTLE
Ground Floor Plan

Re-Drawn From Dimensions Taken In 1949

FIGURE 10

East Cowes Castle

At about this time [1] a second and more grand entrance was constructed to the estate from the south - eastern corner, probably along the line of an old footpath or road. The bordering estate of Osborne had been completely remodelled by Queen Victoria and Prince Albert who had commissioned Thomas Cubitt to complete the works. He had provided a grand arch as a frontispiece entrance to the royal estate from the high road, just opposite this corner of the castle estate. So, in keeping with the distinguished local improvements a Gothic lodge known as 'Southgate Lodge' was constructed opposite the Sovereigns entrance to Osborne.

The lodge; formed over the hollow of an old earthworks or quarry, featured castellated walls and turrets and was constructed of finely rendered brickwork. The accommodation arranged on two levels, around a large central arch through which carriages passed, provided a *porte-cochère* with access to each side of the building from within the arch. Below this level were basement rooms divided by an embankment over which the road passed, and through which, was a tunnel to provide access from side to side. The archway was secured by a large ornamental gate and portcullis emanating from the upper arch. On each side to the front of the lodge crenellated walls, terminated in large square pillars, formed an imposing crescent.

From 1861 until 1933 generations of the Vereker family lived at East Cowes Castle and were the last line of owner occupants. During 1883 major additions were made to the castle, *figure 10*, reconstructed from dimensions taken in 1949, indicates the extensive scale of the work undertaken. The entrance porch 'which projected considerably in advance of the main building' was reduced in length and the curtain walling forming the original courtyard and kitchen screen was removed. The kitchen area was extended and a new bakery with a small first floor room above, incorporating a circular tower within its north-eastern wall, was constructed as a separate building. This in turn was connected to the kitchen block by crenellated walling forming a small courtyard. Other rooms on two levels were provided at the rear of the gallery wall within this complex.

The work was executed to a high standard with original detail maintained and matching materials used throughout. The revisions somewhat interrupting Nash's compact picturesque lines, the entrance front to the building taking on a more balanced but formal appearance.

At some time between 1883 and 1898 East Cowes Castle Farm was built. An unsurprising red brick cottage and adjoining dairy, with various farm outbuildings. Situated to the south of the castle and utilising, to good effect, the well watered fertile meadows of the sloping parkland.

The Vereker family, whilst resident at East Cowes were generous benefactors to the local church and town. The castle was regularly open to visitors and outings and fêtes held there. In 1887 Viscount Gort donated land to the town for the Jubilee recreation ground. Approximately four and a half acres, south-west of the Castle and separated from the estate by the new high road, Albert Grove, was given.

During 1933 the remaining members of the Vereker family sold the castle and estate to a syndicate of Cowes business men and moved from the island.

---

1 - *Parish records of 1850 indicate a rate levied against East Cowes Castle for the Lodge.*

25. Shannon Castle : from an engraving by T. Barber c1845.

26A. Shannon Castle : from an engraving by T.Shepherd c1845.

26B. The restored clock mechanism from East Cowes Castle manufactured in 1819, the clock
face not shown in illustrations of the castle until about 1845.

27. The conservatory at East Cowes Castle : an 1884 photograph taken from the lawn.

28. East Cowes Castle entrance front north : a photograph taken in 1911.

29. East Cowes Castle entrance front south : a photograph taken during the early part of the century showing the extensive alterations to the kitchen block completed in 1883.

30. East Cowes castle, view to the north : a photograph taken in August 1884 from the castle roof above the drawing room

31. East Cowes Castle, view to the south : a photograph taken in 1884 from the kitchen tower, the twin towers of Osborne can be seen in the distance. The detail of the long conservatory roof, regents room and stable block can also be seen.

35. East Cowes Castle, the approach from North Lodge : a photograph taken in the Spring of 1934

36. East Cowes Castle, the approach from Southgate Lodge : the beautiful setting of the castle in mature woodland, a photograph taken in 1934.

3

DECLINE

The new owners of East Cowes Castle continued the tradition introduced by the Earl of Shannon almost one hundred years earlier of opening the grounds to visitors and the upkeep of the formal and kitchen gardens were maintained accordingly. Tea rooms were opened in the castle with a small part of the building given over to accommodation. The fabric of the building at this stage was beginning to show deterioration, not surprising with a conceptual structure of the type and size. Regular investment in building maintenance was a necessity but over the following years circumstances dictated that this investment would not be made.

The clouds of war were gathering over Europe during the 1930's and some little while after the out-break of World War II the buildings and grounds were requisitioned by the War Office in the interests of the country's war effort. Soldiers were billeted at the castle on two occasions, and together with the lack of proper building maintenance, the decline was accelerated. There are accounts of doors and orna-mental panelling torn down to be burned in the castle fireplaces to provide cheer for its estranged occupants. If true, this no doubt would have hastened the inevitable. A subsequent photographic survey [1] undertaken after the war during 1949, did in fact confirm, that in the short period of ten years the building had become a disintegrating shell. More importantly the overall condition was close to being beyond economic restoration.

The situation did not improve during the early 1950's, as the building was open to the skies and subject to widespread vandalism and theft of what materials and fittings could be extracted from the derelict castle. Consequently during 1955 demolition work was put in hand.

For some reason, the contractor who used explosives to demolish the centre section of the castle, includ-ing, the offices, the billiards-room and library, partly cleared the rubble and promptly left the site. Sadly at about this time the beautiful mature woodland to the north and south of the castle, so painstakingly set out by Nash, possibly with Reptons assistance, was cut down. The cleared areas were cultivated and planted as a soft fruit farm, with some minor tidying up and conversion of the Stable Block as the farm office.

This venture did not prove economically viable as during 1958 the entire East Cowes Castle Estate was sold to Mr Arthur Guy for the princely sum of £1,000! He had intentions of making safe the part demolished building, reopening the tea rooms and ultimately developing the park as an eighteen hole golf course. The proposition was imaginative but the task impossible and by the early 1960's the site was sold again, this time to property developers. By 1963 the castle had been completely demolished followed soon afterwards by Southgate Lodge. The stone was dispersed to building sites throughout the Island to be used for less grand purposes.

1 - Photographic Survey by Mr B.Mason of the National Building Record.
  (now the Royal Commission on the Historic Monuments of England).

East Cowes Castle

Nothing whatever remains of East Cowes Castle today, a stark open space fringed by untidy trees marks the place where once stood Nash's castellated baronial mansion with its high romantic battlements. There is a fragment of masonry cleft between the roots of a tree, probably part of the north-eastern terrace relief wall, from where, in Nash's time there were panoramic views across sloping parkland to the sea beyond. Today this view is somewhat changed, modern housing covering the slopes and the view to the near shore obscured by stark industrial buildings which clutter the waters edge. A little apart from the open space and to the north, reached by a modern road which marks the line of the old castle drive, is the sole reminder of Nash's work here, North Lodge. Recently sympathetically restored and extended, Nash's rustic *cottage orné* contrasting sharply with the modern practical houses that surround it.

If searching for reasons why this radiant example of castle-house architecture has been reduced to nothing, one might consider Nash's ultimate state of affairs and professional standing. If he had retired at the peak of his success, if there had been a natural heir and if the title so eagerly sought and deserved had been conferred. Alternatively, was the failure of the Botanical Gardens scheme, that might have maintained East Cowes as a fashionable resort, a contributory cause? Was the rapid consequential growth of industry with its ever pressing demand for development land the primary cause? All conjecture perhaps, more a combination of these factors and that during the austere 1930's no one was prepared to fund the upkeep of a pretentious castle-house that was no longer *à la mode*

History, therefore, records that a once famous architect buried in relative obscurity at East Cowes, lived in a sham castle that no longer exists. Yet Nash's resplendent show house had dominated the eastern skyline of Cowes for one hundred and sixty years, but the architecture and the builder have almost been forgotten, relics of another time, swept away on the winds of change.

37. Cowes, an aerial view taken 27 June 1942 : this war time photograph indicates the preserved boundary of the castle estate and little indication of the development to follow. To the south the circular landscape is the remains of the East Cowes Botanical Gardens.

38. East Cowes Castle entrance front : the unkempt entrance and surrounds in 1949.

39. East Cowes Castle, north-west front : the desolation of the north-west elevation in 1949.

40. East Cowes Castle, view to the south from the octagon tower : this 1949 photograph indicating the building open to the skies. The conventional pitched roofs can be seen behind the ornamental battlements.

41. East Cowes Castle, view from the octagonal tower to the north in 1949 : the coursed rubble masonry of the staircase tower appears in good condition in this photograph. The access road from North Lodge can be seen in the top lefthand corner of the picture.

42. East Cowes Castle, view from the octagon tower to the north-west in 1949: Nash's mature parkland and the mainland beyond, depicted in this September photograph.

43. East Cowes Castle, staircase tower : this 1949 photograph still displaying features described by Joseph Farington in 1817. The walls may have once been part of an old windmill.

44. East Cowes Castle, the billiards-room : Nash's ornate pendantal plasterwork all but destroyed as shown in this 1949 photograph.

45. East Cowes Castle, the drawing-room in 1949 : a sorry scene, virtually all reusable material torn from the building.

46. East Cowes Castle, conservatory entrance from the lawn in 1949 the long conservatory once the most beautiful feature completely overgrown. The rendered masonry does, however, look to be in good condition

47. East Cowes Castle, stable block in 1949 : restored and used as the farm office during the 1950's.

48. East Cowes Castle, view from the south c1958 : Nash's mature woodland has almost disappeared in this picture but the setting is still picturesque.

49. East Cowes Castle from the east c1958 : a view across the blackberry fields, after the centre section of the building had been demolished.

50. Southgate Lodge c1964 : the decaying building just prior to demolition.

51. North Lodge c1964 : the remaining mark of Nash's country estate, the beautiful parkland can be seen to the left of the cottage.

52. East Cowes 1963 : an aerial view of the castle estate taken on 27 April 1963. By this time the building had been completely demolished and the site cleared. The development of John Nash Avenue can be seen at centre of the picture.

53. The site where East Cowes Castle once stood.

4

CASTLE-HOUSE CYCLE

ash's houses and castles are considered a most important contribution to British architecture and rank with his better known metropolitan terraces and street scenes. It is in these houses that we see Nash at his most creative and unrestrained, not as the speculative builder or town planner, but a successful architect whose talents and achievements led to the patronage of the landed gentry. So much so, that between the years 1792 and 1812 Nash had evolved the most enviable practice in England, building or remodelling forty mansions and numerous embellishments to country estates in the form of cottages, lodges and farms throughout the Kingdoms of England, Wales and Ireland. During one of those prolific years, as Nash told Farington, he had 'travelled in the three Kingdoms eleven thousand miles in the year and expended £1500 in chase hire', advising and supervising the work associated with his commissions. A tremendous undertaking in the late eighteenth or early nineteenth century requiring the utmost in physical energy and determination.

Although Nash professed to dislike working in Gothic, his greatest successes came from its form. He is quoted as saying 'one window takes more trouble in designing than two houses ought to'. Gothic was the popular order and the corner stone of his successful country house period. Of the work completed during this cycle, there are large Gothic mansions, stuccoed classical and villa style houses and of course the castle-houses. Nash's commitments towards the Regent's grand metropolitan improvements effectively brought the country house period to a close and although Gothic was still eminently fashionable and used extensively elsewhere, it was completely absent from his Regents Park and Regent Street developments.

The castle-houses, considered in more detail here, and analogous to East Cowes, are stone built castellated mansions with pretentious towers and turrets designed to give an illusion of grandeur, but with the most Classical of interiors. Some were heroic and beautifully sited, as was East Cowes, others dull and forbidding, but all combined to give an impressive picture of Nash's attempt to produce his picturesque ideal on a grand scale. From the humble beginnings of the little symmetrical house on the rocks and the association with the antecedent Downton, East Cowes Castle was conceived, initiating in its wake a generation of castle-houses. Without doubt, if Nash had not been drawn toward the prestigious grand scale works, his success would have been assured through his country house architecture, both exemplified and consolidated throughout the castle-house cycle.

CHRONOLOGICAL LISTING OF NASH'S CASTLE-HOUSES

1. East Cowes Castle, I.W 1798-1834
2. Luscombe Castle, Dawlish, Devon 1800-1804
3. Killymoon Castle, Cookstown, Co.Tyrone c1802
4. Childwall Hall, Childwall, Lancashire 1805 - 1811
5. Garnstone Castle, Weobley, Herefordshire c1806
6. Kilwaughter Castle, Near Larne, Co.Antrim c1807
7. Ravensworth Castle, Near Gateshead Co.Durham c1807
8. Caerhays Castle, St.Michael Caerhays, Cornwall 1808
9. West Grinstead Park, Sussex c1809
10. Knepp Castle, Sussex c1809
11. Lough Cutra Castle, Gort, Co.Galway c1815
12. Shanbally Castle,Co.Tipperary 1818-1819

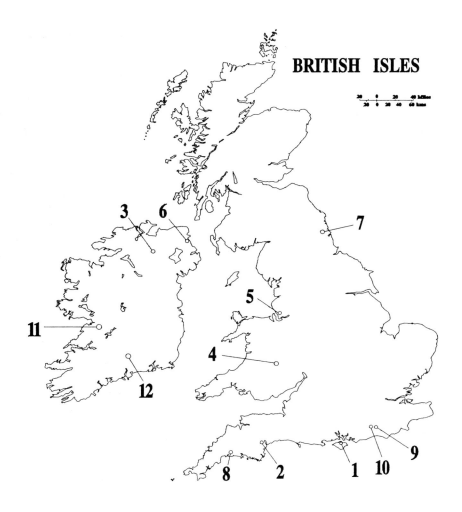

BRITISH ISLES

Castle-House Cycle

1.   EAST COWES CASTLE, I.W. 1798-1834

Nash's country seat where assertive architecture was pre-eminent, it lacked the practicality of his later galleried castle-houses

Because Nash's country house evolved over many years it does not merit direct comparison with other houses in the cycle. Its initial compactness can be likened to Luscombe but its final elevations were quite unlike those of its successors.

East Cowes was not a large house overall although the dimensions between its extremities in completed form, *figure 9*, were vast. It did not contain the great series of rooms as did the later great castle-houses and the Nashes accommodation was virtually a self contained appartment above the dining and drawing-rooms. The remainder of the house was given over to entertainment and show, this was achieved to great affect. The principal rooms being the smaller of the conservatories, that could double as a ball-room and the northern end of the long conservatory, in which the Regent Street Gallery was ultimately installed.

Special guests were accommodated in the regents room and suite and others in the first and second floor accommodation throughout the castle. The completion of the octogon tower did provide four large rooms on the various levels but the access was somewhat restricted. During the years of high living every available room in the house must have been used.

2.   LUSCOMBE CASTLE, DAWLISH, DEVON 1800-1804

A castellated house designed for Charles Hoare the Banker.

Repton completed his survey in the red book in June 1799 and in selecting the site pronounced 'a castle which by blending a chaste correctness of proportion with bold irregularity and outline'. He then introduced Mr Nash, 'my ingenious friend, who without losing sight of the internal arrangements, disposition, or convenience, has given the house an outline which from its chaste simplicity must always please the Eye of Taste. Its very irregularity will give it consequence, while the offices and mere walls which in a modern building it would be essential to conceal, by partaking of the character of the Castle, will extend its Scite and make it an apparently considerable pile of a building.'

So much for the pre-amble, the result was indeed picturesque and pleasant, irregular and castellated. Repton's site was located between two lightly wooded hills against a background of enriched forest, the approach providing an abrupt introduction to the mansion cleft in the niche of the landscape.

The impression is one of quaintness rather than ruggedness. Nash's original plan did not allow for the oversize bay window added after completion and it is as a result, extraneous. Most of the interior details are classical and the fine staircase incorporating Nash's favourite 'S balusters' in the hand rail, is lit by a large window with Gothic tracery.

3.   KILLYMOON CASTLE CO.TYRONE c1802

A small castle built for Colonel William Stewart.

Killymoon was picturesquely sited on high ground adjacent to a fast flowing river. Nash's composition of rooms used in many of his larger country houses are elliptical, octagonal and square in shape. George Repton's sketch book indicates a romantic moonlit castellated building with arched windows and featuring a prominent tall porch incorporating three distinctive Norman arches.

A narrow vaulted corridor led up to a vestibule with an almost flat vaulted plaster ceiling and beyond via a narrow pointed arch,into the dismal stair-case hall, illuminated only by a tinted glass lantern. Other interior features were of inventive Gothic, some finished in rich polished oak. There are references in Nash's diary of 1832 to correspondence with Mr Stewart of Killymoon regarding repairs to the building.

The house cost £80,000 to build and was sold during the 1950's in total ruin for £100.

4   CHILDWALL HALL, NEAR LIVERPOOL, LANCASHIRE 1805-1811

A castellated house built for Bamber Gascoyne, Member of Parliament for Liverpool.

Childwall Hall although considered as the second of Nash's least interesting compositions was built of red sandstone with square, round and octagonal towers and did possess a striking silhouette reminiscent of Knepp Castle.

The octagonal tower contained a study on the ground floor on the axis of the long gallery, at the far end of which was a stair climbing in three flights. The gallery ceiling was flat panelled and adorned with diagonally arranged squares supported at the wall joints by plaster fan - vaults emanating from mural colonettes which became pendantal where the stair-case emerged. The library windows were fitted with ingenious shutters which, when drawn, were completely concealed within the upper wall recesses.

The house eventually passed to the Marquess of Salisbury, ultimately became a golf Club and was demolished during 1949.

5   GARNSTONE, NEAR LEOMINSTER HEREFORDSHIRE c1806

A large castle -house built for Samuel Peploe.

Described as Tudor Gothic and built of green sandstone in seven-inch courses, Garnstone was the first of four great castle-houses designed by Nash, but considered his least interesting.

A massive stair-case tower was lit by a large lantern and high level abbreviated six light traceried windows. From this tower extended a wide gallery sandwiched between two rows of principal rooms.

At a later date the house was much altered including the rebuilding of the stairs. The house was eventually demolished during 1958.

6.   KILWAUGHTER CASTLE, CO.ANTRIM c1807

A Gothic mansion for Edward Jones Agnew incorporating a seventeenth century Castle.

The composition of grouping small towers and turrets around a massive round tower was similar to that employed at West Grinstead and Knepp. The windows all rectangular with labels, were enhanced by wooden tracery and the sandstone sills were enriched by primitive carving of some originality.

The entrance porch, somewhat hidden, to the west of the round tower, led to an inner vestibule and on to a half-octagonal stair-case hall. This contained semi-circular alcoves, one of which gave access to the circular drawing-room. The stair-case hall was panelled with open Gothic tracery and the dining-room enriched with vaulted plaster spandrels with restrained fluting, overall however, the quality of internal details was not good.

The house was stripped of its fittings in 1951 and now lies in ruins.

7.   RAVENSWORTH CASTLE, CO.DURHAM c1807

An ambitious Gothic style house, designed for Sir Thomas Liddell, a successful industrialist of great wealth.

The second of Nash's great castle-houses was built on the site of an earlier Georgian house that incorporated two thirteenth century towers. The original plan for Ravensworth indicated a wide, long gallery consisting of five bays domed in the Classical manner and leading via a lobby to a round stair-case tower. This also gave access to the drawing-room and Gothic library, the latter containing pinnacled book cases and a vaulted ceiling, supported on corbels. The main suite of living rooms was situated on a parallel axis to the gallery.

The exterior elevations were all complex unco-ordinated and rather uninviting. The house was much altered during construction and was not completed in Nash's life time.

The house, once used as a school, was enlarged during the 1840's, eventually fell into decay and was demolished during 1953.

8.   CAERHAYS CASTLE, ST MICHAEL CAERHAYS, CORNWALL 1808

A Gothic house built for John Bettesworth.

Considered as the most successful of Nash's great castle-houses it is constructed of squared rubble in simple Gothic style and commands magnificent views across park lands and the Cornish seascape. Rugged yet noble in appearance, the composition is arranged around its large round towers against a woodland setting. The castle was originally hidden from the sea until extensive landscaping in Victorian times removed the offending hilltop.

The ground floor is on the usual gallery concept, vaulted and top lit by a galleried opening, which leads to an impressive double return stair-case, behind an arch supported on classical corbels. A lobby providing access to a little circular closet and onto the library and circular drawing-room. The main suite of rooms is arranged in parallel with the gallery, around the walls of which is an ornamented railed balcony, this duplicating an inner upstairs corridor. The internal details are a mixture of Gothic and Classical and although quite sparse, do contain Classical mouldings of a modest nature.

There is a stable courtyard, a later addition, approached through a broad arch, built to conform to the original details of the house. A defensive terrace terminated in a round watch tower completes the exterior ornamentation.

9. WEST GRINSTEAD PARK, SUSSEX c1809

A large castellated house built for Walter Burell the younger son of the Sussex historian.

Designed around a large round tower and built on a level site amidst the gently undulating Sussex countryside, Nash's composition had a wild romantic air set within the meadow and bracken. Constructed of Limestone cut to brick size, its original elevations were very picturesque, but later additions were ill conceived and completely altered the original plain grim outline.

The original house was of compact gallery design with the main rooms on the east side. The interior was very elegant and featured an impressive double return stair-case and circular dining-room decorated with a cornice of tiny groins and descending wall ribs. There were curved recesses with side tables and four centred arches and mirrors all finished in neat Gothic detail. The library within a square tower was adjacent to the drawing room and had a round arched loggia.

Two of the main bedrooms contained good marble chimney pieces one white and lavender coloured the other white and richly carved.

The house was ill treated during the Second World War, unoccupied for many years and finally demolished in 1970.

10. KNEPP CASTLE, SUSSEX c1809

A Gothic mansion built for Sir Charles Burrell, Father of the House of Commons.

Upon the success of West Grinstead was based Nash's commission at Knepp. More grandiose than West Grinstead and less compact, the building is cement rendered and sited in a picturesque park with a lake nearby.

Nash's design is based around a large round stair-case tower with Gothic windows, which connects through a square lobby with the inner hall, saloon and dining-room, similar to the original plan for Ravensworth. The entrance front to the house is most impressive with four identical towers. The out buildings arranged around a courtyard, are situated to the north-west.

In 1904 a severe fire destroyed much of the interior, now fully restored but somewhat altered in the restoration. The house is still in the ownership of the Burrell family.

11. LOUGH CUTRA CASTLE, CO.GALWAY c1815

A Gothic Limestone house built above the shores of Lough Cutra for the Right Hon.Charles Vereker, Member of Parliament for Limerick.

Charles Vereker who became Lord Gort in 1817, so admired Nash's castle that he commissioned him to build a castle based on East Cowes at Gort in the remote and beautiful west of Ireland. The castle stands on a terrace blasted out of the rocky slopes leading down to the lough and does resemble Nash's vanished castle. It enjoys magnificent views across the lough to the unspoilt richly wooded countryside beyond. The great octagonal tower is however much larger than at East Cowes, the castle design less rambling, a compact version of Ravensworth.

The gallery is more of a centre feature here, being simply a long vaulted Gothic hall with the main entrance to the house in the middle of one side. At one end a broad arch leads to the stair-case tower, which accesses the bedroom landing, lit by three circular domes. The stair-case made of oak, is of Gothic design and although pleasing is less spectacular than most of Nash's stair-cases. Alongside the hall is the drawing-room, this enters at one end the great octagonal tower and at the other a semi octagon room which forms a bay window overlooking the lough. On the axis of this room is a second octagon tower, to the landward, over topped by its own circular stair-case turret.

The drawing-room has a rich Gothic cornice but the original marble chimney piece has been replaced. Two alcoves at the north end once contained decorative wood and plaster work, but this has been removed. The drawing-room and dining-room are en-suite, linked by a vaulted ante room originally containing great double doors.

The Stable Block which contains some of the original fittings from the house is now a separate residence. There are two distinctive castellated lodges to the estate both believed to have been designed by Nash.

The castle is semi-derelict but a long term restoration seems to be in progress, the east wing and giant clock tower, added in 1856 have been demolished restoring the original fiercely castellated silhouette.

12. SHANBALLY CASTLE, CO.TIPPERARY 1818-1819

A great Gothic composition built for the Earl of Lismore, the work completed by A.Hargreaves.

Shanbally was the last and most accomplished of Nash's series of castle-houses, both in plan and detail. The original undated plans are at the R.I.B.A. and the building was designed when Nash was heavily involved with the metropolitan improvements and was unable to visit Ireland to supervise the works.

The rather subdued entrance front contrasted sharply with the spectacular south face where large round and hexagonal towers terminated the great sequence of Gothic windows and tracery of the conservatory.

The detail of the Gothic interior was tastefully conceived and included prominent marble chimney pieces. The entrance hall, known as the gallery was vaulted and top lit by a series of rose shaped lights. A great archway led to a most splendid Nash double return stair-case with a refined vaulted Gothic ceiling. The hexagonal dining-room connected to an oval drawing-room by a square ante-room and from the drawing room a series of rooms, including the library and conservatory stretched along the south side. This series of rooms was completed by two small hexagonal rooms and there were other rooms of considerable size within the ground floor complex.

Shanbally Castle, before years of neglect, was the ultimate example of a Nash galleried castle-house, built of beautifully cut stone and ready to endure the centuries, it was unceremoniously blown up by demolition contractors in March 1960.

54. Luscombe Castle and groundfloor plan : view from the east from an engraving by I.Smith c1815

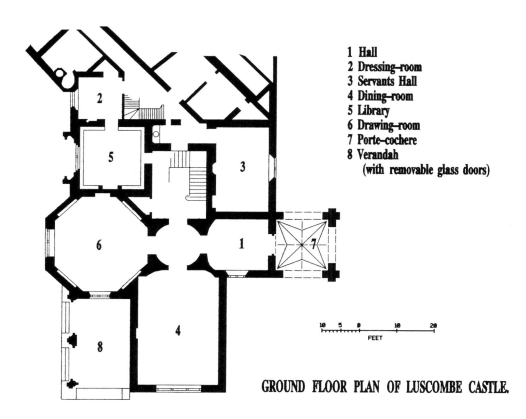

1 Hall
2 Dressing–room
3 Servants Hall
4 Dining–room
5 Library
6 Drawing–room
7 Porte–cochere
8 Verandah
(with removable glass doors)

FEET

GROUND FLOOR PLAN OF LUSCOMBE CASTLE.

55. Killymoon Castle and groundfloor plan : a photograph taken in the 1930's.

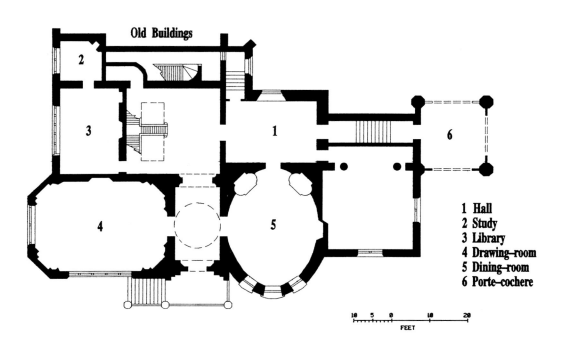

Old Buildings

1 Hall
2 Study
3 Library
4 Drawing–room
5 Dining–room
6 Porte–cochere

FEET

GROUND FLOOR PLAN OF KILLYMOON

56. Garnstone Castle : Nash's Tudor Gothic castle-house.

57. Childwall Hall : accredited for its fine silhouette only. From an engraving after a drawing by
   J.P.Neale.

58. Kilwaughter Castle and groundfloor plan : a somewhat grim outline, a photograph taken
    shortly before its degradation.

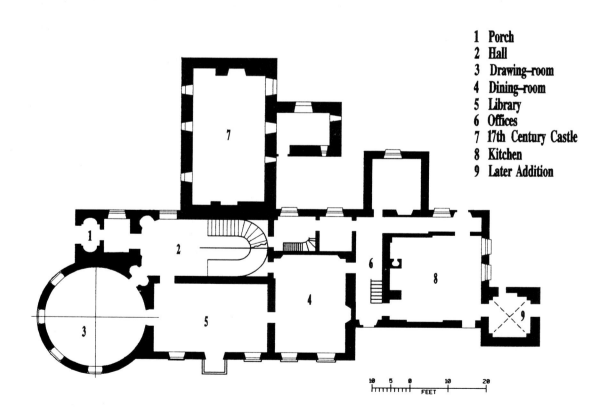

1 Porch
2 Hall
3 Drawing–room
4 Dining–room
5 Library
6 Offices
7 17th Century Castle
8 Kitchen
9 Later Addition

FEET

GROUND FLOOR PLAN OF KILWAUGHTER CASTLE

59. Ravensworth Castle and groundfloor plan : much altered from Nash's proposals in its building.

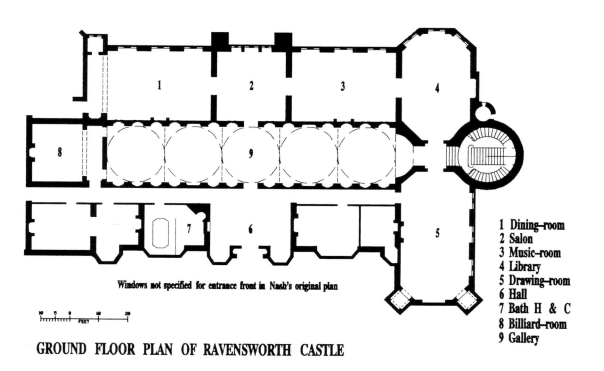

Windows not specified for entrance front in Nash's original plan

1 Dining–room
2 Salon
3 Music–room
4 Library
5 Drawing–room
6 Hall
7 Bath H & C
8 Billiard–room
9 Gallery

GROUND FLOOR PLAN OF RAVENSWORTH CASTLE

60A   Caerhays Castle : Nash's last surviving great castle-house. View from the sea.

60B.   Caerhays Castle : The   *porte-cochère*

61. West Grinstead Park and groundfloor plan : from an engraving based on a drawing by
G.S.Repton.

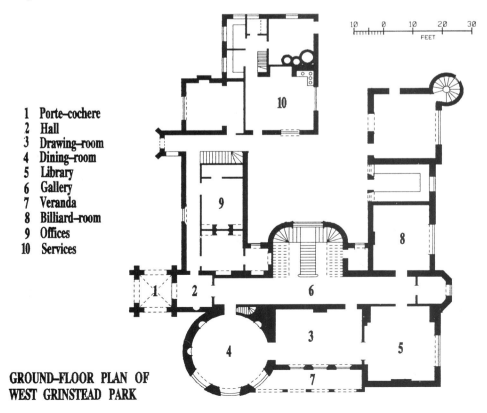

1   Porte–cochere
2   Hall
3   Drawing–room
4   Dining–room
5   Library
6   Gallery
7   Veranda
8   Billiard–room
9   Offices
10   Services

FEET

**GROUND–FLOOR PLAN OF
WEST GRINSTEAD PARK**

62. Knepp Castle and groundfloor plan : Nash's imposing entrance front features four identical towers.

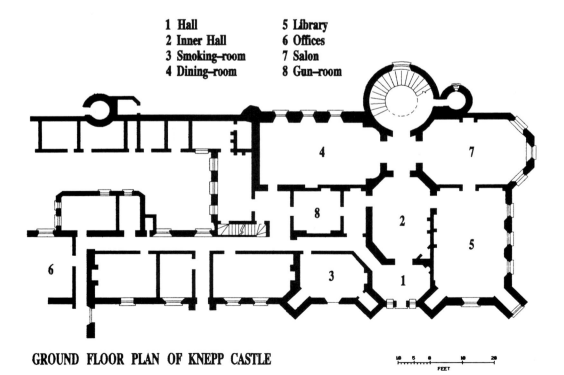

1 Hall   5 Library
2 Inner Hall   6 Offices
3 Smoking–room   7 Salon
4 Dining–room   8 Gun–room

GROUND FLOOR PLAN OF KNEPP CASTLE

FEET

63A. Lough Cutra Castle : a view from across the lough. The octagonal and square towers to the extreme left are Victorian additions.

63B. Lough Cutra Castle : the massive octagon tower.

64. Shanbally Castle : considered the most accomplished of Nash's castle-houses, it contained a great series of classical rooms.

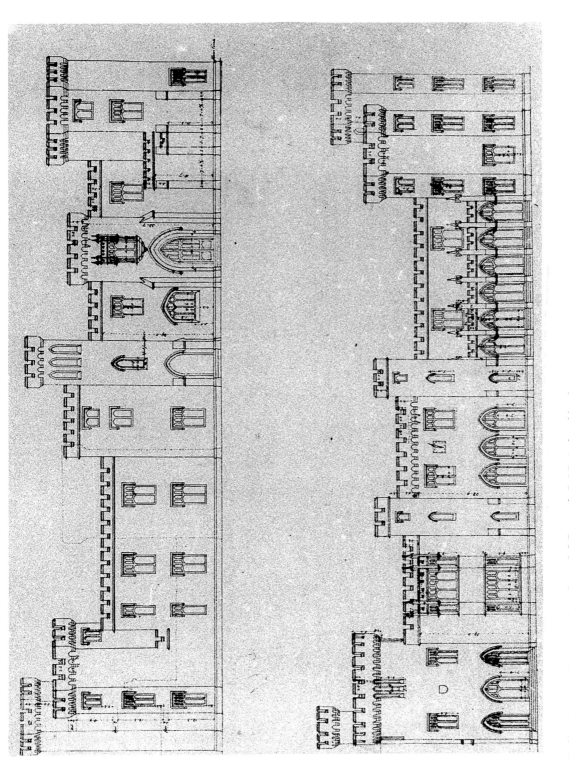

65. Shanbally Castle : elevations from G.S.Repton's R.I.B.A.sketchbook.

66. Shanbally Castle : entrance front and   Porte-cochère

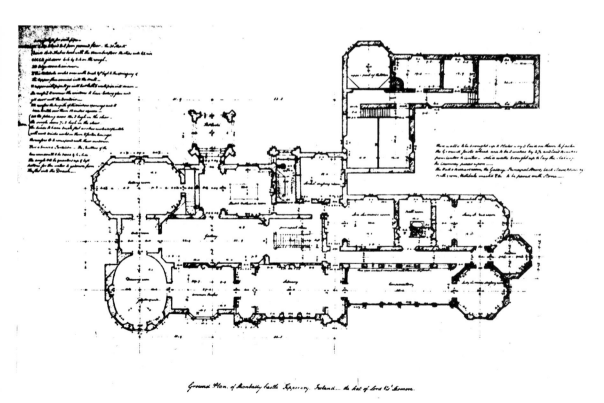

67. Shanbally Castle : plan view from G.S.Repton's R.I.B.A.sketchbook.

5

THE ISLE OF WIGHT ARCHITECT

Through Nash's long association with the Isle of Wight and as his country retreat, it is perhaps not surprising that outside of London the Island represents the most concentrated area of his work. The commissions undertaken include rustic cottages, public buildings and grand country houses, in all, forming a microcosm of his work throughout the Kingdoms.

The excellent catalogue compiled over a period of twelve years by the late Michael Mansbridge [1] has incorporated many previously unknown commissions and together with my own research, I have attempted to detail the substantiated Isle of Wight works. There are no doubt others, many local buildings seem to bear the hallmark of Nash and in the fullness of time and as more information is gathered the list will lengthen.

The result of Nash's first visit during 1793 may not have proved fruitful but the contacts established rewarded both Nash and Repton with local commissions from 1797, before the commencement of construction of East Cowes Castle. Whilst resident on the Island Nash gave freely of his services and undertook two notable public commissions at Newport; the Isle of Wight Institution (9), 1811 and the Guildhall (13), 1814. For the latter The Corporation passed a vote of thanks 'for the very elegant and masterly plans --- which in the most liberal and flattering manner, he (Nash) presented to The Corporation'. Nash was elected a free Burgess of the Borough for his services.

1 - Mansbridge 1991

CHRONOLOGICAL LISTING OF NASH'S ISLE OF WIGHT WORKS

1. *St.Johns, Ryde 1797-1799*
2. *East Cowes Castle 1798-1834*
3. *Northwood House, alterations, church and lodges 1801-1829*
4. *Orchard Cottage, Niton c1805*
5. *Osborne Cottage, East Cowes c1805*
6. *Elm Cottage, adjacent to North Lodge East Cowes.c1805*
7. *Nunwell House, Brading 1805-1807*
8. *Hamstead and Heathfield 1806 - 1832*
9. *Isle of Wight Institution, Newport 1811*
10. *St.Mildred's Church, Whippingham c1813*
11. *Westover House, Calbourne 1813-1815*
12. *Hill Grove, Bembridge 1814*
13. *The Guildhall, Newport 1814*
14. *St.Mildred's Rectory, Whippingham 1819*
15. *Fountain Inn, West Cowes 1823*
16. *Hippisley House, West Cowes 1825*
17. *Holy Trinity Church, Bembridge 1827*
18. *St.James Church, East Cowes 1831-1833*
19. *Barton Manor Farm Cottage, undated*
20. *Spring Hill, East Cowes, undated.*
21. *Villa for Lord Belfast, West Cowes c1832*

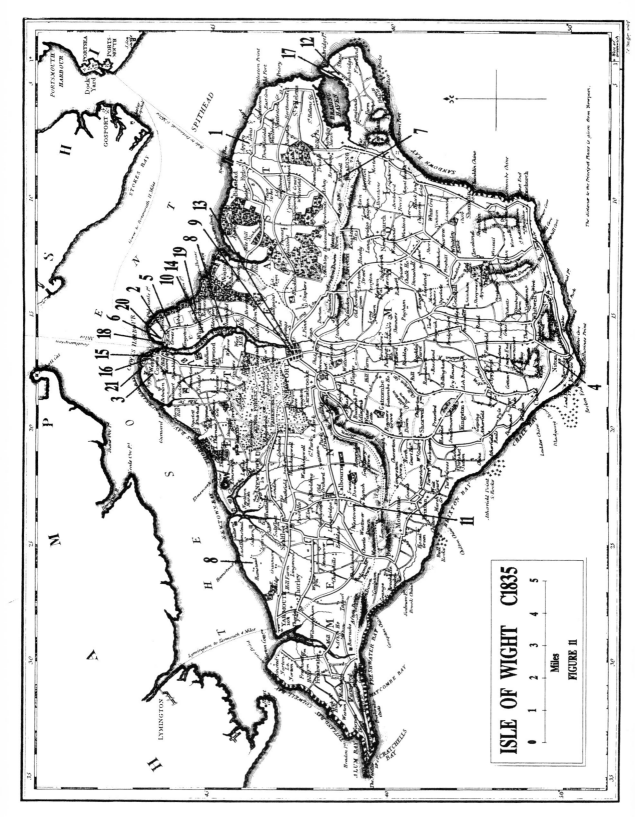

ISLE OF WIGHT C1835

Miles
0 1 2 3 4 5

FIGURE II

1. ST.JOHN'S RYDE 1797-1799

Edward Simeon purchased the estate of St.John's in 1796 and commissioned Humphrey Repton to landscape the parkland. Repton incorporated a new estate entrance in his replanning, adorned by a pair of rustic cottages of stone construction[1], with thatched roofs and large round headed windows facing the public road. Completed during the middle years of the Nash, Repton partnership, it is most likely that Nash designed the cottages and that George Repton re-drew them as a training exercise, after joining the Nash practice in 1802.

On the far side of the estate, close to the Solent shore a castellated marina incorporating a bandstand was built, from which the parading public could be entertained on Sunday afternoons. Although constructed about the same time as the cottages the design cannot be directly attributed to Nash or Repton.

1 - Mansbridge 1991

3. NORTHWOOD HOUSE, CHURCH AND LODGES 1801-1829

George Ward the owner of the Debourne and Bellevue Estates at West Cowes and as an extremely successful and wealthy property speculator engaged Nash to carry out many improvements to his estates. The men became great friends and by 1802 when Nash had completed the first elevations at East Cowes Castle, neighbours. Nash and Ward had much in common, similar in age, both speculators and the fashionable new rich. The surviving Nash diaries indicate the very close relationship between the Nashes and Wards, this after Ward's death in 1829, had continued with his sons and grandchildren. The men were also business associates, notably in 1811 when George Ward and his son combined with Nash on the managing committee of the Regents Canal Company.

George Repton's R.I.B.A. sketch book indicates a block of four cottages and a further cottage and trellis alcove for Mr G Ward at Northwood. The block of cottages is believed to have been incorporated in the present Egypt Cottages and the other building has not been identified. Sketches of a thatched cottage and gazebo and store appear in George Repton's Brighton sketch book, the former of which is known to be Debourne Lodge. The companion piece adjacent to the lodge, known as the Round House is also attributed to Nash but does not replicate the R.I.B.A. sketch book illustration.

During the early 1800's the Bellevue Estate was renamed Northwood Park and Nash was commissioned around 1807 to completely remodel the estate mansion, Northwood House. Nash's design provided a Classical house of generous proportion sharing elemental features of his earlier work at Harpton Court (1805) and much later work at Carlton Gardens (1827). During 1811 and 1822 further work was carried out which included a study, domestic offices and three bedrooms above, accessed by an oval staircase. The later work included the conversion of a stable block into additional bedrooms. In 1837 a large domed annex was added to the house, the architect was believed to have been Charles Lee who had trained in Nash's office.

Across the park from the house stands St Mary's Church, enlarged by Nash during 1811 at a cost of £3,000 and enhanced with a slender tower at the base of which is the Ward family mausoleum. The main body of the church was rebuilt during 1867 but the tower, standing at the west end , remained. It is square in form with top corner *antefixa* and high belfry openings adorned with inset Doric columns. The base of the tower which houses the mausoleum has stylized pediments with further *antefixa* over a Gothic arch, inside are the monuments to the Ward family.

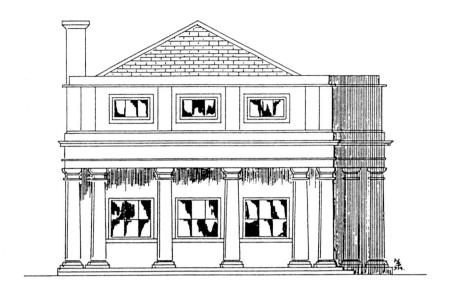

LODGE AT NORTHWOOD PARK, COWES I.O.W.

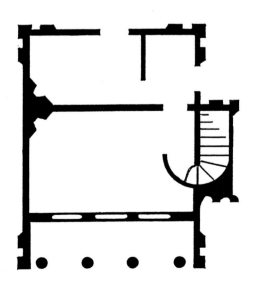

PLAN

**LODGE AT NORTHWOOD PARK
COWES**
Two such Lodges were built
for Mr. G. Ward.

FIGURE 12

66

Barber[1] comments 'The style of this tower is certainly more singular than tasteful; the architect was John Nash Esq.'

Immediately to the east of the church is a Classical lodge constructed of stone with a prominent Doric order to the front elevation, it survives a similar lodge to the north which has long been demolished. A Gothic arch once stood at the main entrance to the estate close by the lodge, designed by Nash, it was demolished during the 1930's.

1 - Barber 1845

4.   ORCHARD COTTAGE, NITON c1805

Orchard Cottage[1] is believed to have been the country retreat of James MacKenzie Esq whose main residence was at Cowes. The plan in George Repton's R.I.B.A. sketchbook indicates a simple arrangement of an eating-room, 'parlour' and kitchen accessed from a small stair-case hall. The first floor accommodation comprised of two large and three small bedrooms. The exact site of the cottage is not known.

1 - Mansbridge 1991

5.   OSBORNE COTTAGE, EAST COWES c1805

Osborne Cottage was a large *cottage-orné* that stood facing the high road just south-east of East Cowes Castle. The half timbered front was an unusual feature for Nash and the presentations in George Repton's R.I.B.A. sketchbook show two plans differing only in detail, a drawing-room, library and kitchen being the principle rooms.

The cottage was purchased by Queen Victoria as a residence for the Clerk of the Works whilst Osborne House was under construction. In 1856 it was demolished and replaced by a large Victorian house also fronting the old high road. Unusually, this house is now situated with its rear elevation to the main road, as Queen Victoria closed the old high road in 1898 to improve the privacy at Osborne.

The building is now a residential home for the elderly.

6.   ELM COTTAGE, EAST COWES c1805

George Brannon's engraving of 15 November 1820 depicts a thatched two storey rustic cottage, known as Mr Lamberts cottage. The building[1] stood across the high road adjacent to Nash's North Lodge entrance to his country estate. The pretty cottage had a triple arched front elevation with a pinnacled roof and central chimney.

Nash's diary of 1832 records dining at Mr Lamberts on Saturday 6 October and the 1834 accounts list for the Parish of East Cowes indicates the property to be in the possession of Mrs Lambert.

The building has long disappeared and the site redeveloped and there is no trace of Nash's work.

1 - Summerson 1935 (C4, P87)

7.   NUNWELL HOUSE, BRADING 1805-1807.

Nash was commissioned by Sir William Oglander to design a new house[1] to replace his sixteenth century manor. The architect proposed a galleried house with Classical elevations but this was not executed because during 1807 Sir William inherited Parham House Dorset and at a later stage employed Nash to modernise. Nash did however carry out repairs at Nunwell, including the re-building of the Stable Block which is now the main residence. He also removed the oak panelling from the room occupied by Charles I during his last night of freedom, before his imprisonment in nearby Carisbrooke Castle.

The Manor House is now open to the public.

1 - Mansbridge 1991.

8.   HAMSTEAD AND HEATHFIELD 1806-1832

As at East Cowes, Hamstead was the subject of much alteration during Nash's time. Standing in an elevated position with fine views across the west Solent and Newtown Creek, the site was surrounded by dense woodland some 1½ miles from the Newport - Yarmouth road.

Hamstead is an ancient site recorded on the Domesday map of 1086 and the house and grounds are believed to have been part of an early monastic settlement. The round tower of the house when purchased by Nash bearing a plate dated 1401. The sketch in George Repton's R.I.B.A. sketch book details a considerable cottage style house with a thatched roof incorporating the old round tower, two full length bay windows and an entrance porch. By 1832 however, the tower had been doubled in height and a new projecting gable constructed.

After Nash's death in 1835 Mrs Nash, Ann, Sarah and John Pennethorne lived at Hamstead, later Rose Pennethorne, the unmarried daughter of James also made her home there. The property remained the Isle of Wight home of the Pennethorne family until Rose's death in 1923, but was much altered and enlarged, in the process destroying all of Nash's original work. The house was finally demolished some years ago and a modern building now occupies the site.

There are detailed accounts [1] for the years 1832-3-4 for Nash's business activities at East Cowes Castle, Hamstead and Heathfield Farm. From these, a picture emerges of the operation of Brick and Lime kilns located at East Hamstead just half a mile from Nash's manor-house. There are ledger entries for maintenance of the kilns and transportation of materials to and from the point of manufacture. Nash installed and operated a light railway system between these kilns and a convenient loading area close to the main estate road, along the route of the present road to Lower Hamstead. There was also a road from this point to the Solent shore and may have been a small quay associated with the movement of materials. Today there is no trace of a railway system but the accounts detail 'carting on railroad and unloading' and Nash's diary for September 25 and 26, 1832 indicates visits to the 'rail-road' at Hamstead.

One mile south of Whippingham and approximately 2½ miles from where Nash's castle once stood, is a locality known as Heathfield. In the early nineteenth century this comprised two farms, North and South Heathfield, each with farm buildings close to the Newport high road.

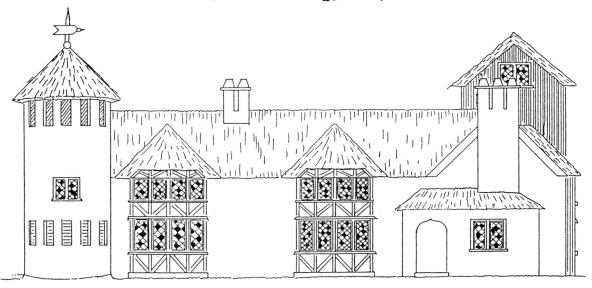

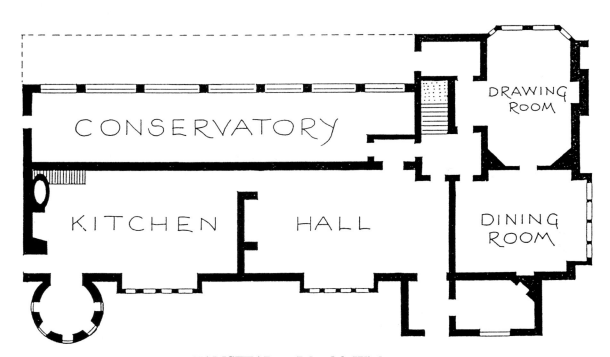

HAMSTEAD   Isle Of Wight.

Nash's first elevations C1806.

FIGURE 13.

In 1778 North Heathfield was leased by William Pike, a Portsmouth brewer from its owners, Winchester College. It is most likely that from 1806 Nash took up this lease and farmed the 100 acres until his death in 1835. The Nash diaries mentioned 'alterations at the farms', but the scope of Nash's work, if any is not recorded.

South of the property is an area known as 'Brickfields corner', so called because of the brick making activities once carried out there and signified by the copious use of red bricks in the surrounding buildings. It is not known if this activity was originated by Nash, complementary to the business at Hamstead, as the surviving Heathfield Farm accounts relate only to farming activities and building work.

In 1843 North Heathfield was purchased by Queen Victoria and added to the Osborne Estate. A pair of substantial Victorian cottages occupy the site of earlier farm cottages, situated close to the main road. Approximately 50 metres to the south east is the site of North Heathfield Farm now blotted out, no trace of Nash's work remains.

1 - Nash Papers

9.   ISLE OF WIGHT INSTITUTION, NEWPORT 1811

The Isle of Wight Institution as designed by Nash consisted of a reading room and a town museum. It is a Classical building executed and detailed in Portland stone with a front elevation of an arcarded colonnade supporting a central pediment via pilasters.

The building is now used for commercial purposes at ground floor level and as a private club on the first floor.

10.   ST.MILDRED'S CHURCH, WHIPPINGHAM c1813

There has been a church on the site of St.Mildred's since the twelfth century and prior to 1813 there was a Norman nave, a thirteenth century chancel, a western tower and saddleback roof dating from the fourteenth century.

Nash reconstructed the church in Gothic style adding two transepts with galleries accessed by external covered stair-ways and a school room at the foot of the tower. The pitched roof of the tower was removed and a timbered spire and pinnacled buttresses added. Belfry openings were installed in the tower to permit the installation of church bells.

In 1855 a new chancel was installed at Queen Victoria's expense for use of the Royal Family, when resident at Osborne, and finally a new church built in 1861 designed by Prince Albert incorporating the new chancel. There is a piece of early Norman sculpture, representing two men on horseback incorporated in the new church wall, the only surviving fragment of the Norman origins.

The present church has two fonts, one originally designed by Nash, constructed of Limestone with a plain head and sunken bowl supported by a fluted Doric column on a stone base. It is detailed as one of three alternative designs in George Repton's R.I.B.A. sketchbook.

11.   WESTOVER HOUSE, CALBORNE 1813 - 1815

Sir Leonard Holmes commissioned Nash to embellish his brick built Georgian house set in beautiful parkland near Brightstone Forest. Nash added a Doric entrance porch flanked by shallow bay windows and a canopied verandah on the southern aspect. Both elevations were decorated with pediments and the house refinished with stucco. Internally the decorations are Classical and an attractive curved staircase is lit by an overhead lantern.

The drive to the house was re-routed to the North via a new ornamental bridge crossing a stream. An octagonal lodge constructed of rubble and flint and a pretty *cottage orné* adorn the estate and both are believed to have been added at this time. There is a letter [1] from Nash to Sir Leonard dated 9 December 1813, dealing with the specification and accounts for Westover.

1 - Mansbridge 1991.

12.   HILLGROVE, BEMBRIDGE 1814

Hillgrove is considered one of the best Classical houses on the Island and is located above the harbour with fine views of the Solent and mainland beyond. It has a square plan with Doric pilasters at each corner and a canted bay with paired Ionic columns at each side of the main entrance way, surmounted by a dome as a central feature. The West front has a full height shallow bow and the service wing to the East is separated from the main building by a deep recess. Built originally for the Earl of Dulcie the building is Grade II listed but has been unoccupied since the 1960's and lies a disintegrating shell.

13.   THE GUILDHALL, NEWPORT 1814.

The second of Nash's public commissions in Newport was another Classical building, faced with stucco and fulfilling the function of market house and Town Hall. The lower level providing the market house and the upper storey a small Council Chamber, Town Clerk's office, Town Hall and Jury closet. The front and side elevations feature arched colonnades the front supporting an Ionic portico and the High Street side a covered Ionic balcony.

The symmetry of the building was disturbed by the erection of a Victorian Clock tower in 1887 commemorating Queen Victoria's Golden Jubilee.

The design recalls Nash's earlier proposals for public buildings and is now known as Newport Town Hall.

14.   ST. MILDRED'S RECTORY, WHIPPINGHAM 1819

Nash is credited[1] with the rebuilding of the rectory, the details of which are shown in George Repton's Brighton sketch book. The ground floor hall which gave access to the dining-room, drawing-room and study also contained the secondary stair-case to the bedroom accommodation above. The substantial building was further enhanced by the addition of a great bay window contributing to the fine western outlook across the river and countryside beyond. The cost of rebuilding was £4,000.

The Reverend Hook is believed to have been the owner, was in residence between 1820 and 1825 and was the local parson at East Cowes. His brother, Theodore Hook was the editor of the satirical paper the *'John Bull'* and was a friend of Nash's for many years.

1 - Mansbridge 1991.

15. FOUNTAIN INN, WEST COWES 1823

The original architect for the Fountain Inn, built in 1813 is unknown, but may have been Nash [1] . Drawings dated 17 April 1823 found among the papers of George Ward, Nash's friend, business associate and neighbour indicate an extension to the building of stables, storage-rooms, a ball-room and coffee-room. The extension was not built and a single storey dining-room substituted. The Fountain Inn, situated on the town quay was part of the public improvements of Cowes erected at the expense of George Ward.

The property is now known as 'The Fountain Hotel'.

1 - Mansbridge 1991.

16. HIPPISLEY HOUSE, WEST COWES 1825

Hippisley House was a Gothic villa sited on West Cowes parade and built for Sir John Coxe-Hippisley. Situated between Cowes Castle and a villa once owned by George IV, its front elevation had two gabled bays between pinnacled buttresses and canted bay windows on the ground floor. The entrance was on the western side adjacent to the Pavilion, which was built in the grounds behind the villa and used as a ball-room.

The pavilion was later converted into Castle Rock House and ultimately became part of the Royal Corinthian Yacht Club. An annex to the Royal Yacht Squadron now occupies the site of the demolished villa.

17. HOLY TRINITY CHURCH, BEMBRIDGE 1827

A simple Gothic church [1] depicted in the Brannon engraving of 1 July 1829 was situated close to the Classical house Hillgrove. Little is known of the design, the building was demolished in 1845 and replaced by the church now standing on the site.

1 - Summerson 1980 (C11, P155).

18. ST.JAMES'S CHURCH, EAST COWES 1831-1833

Nash's simple Gothic church stood across the park from his country house, the foundation stone of which was laid by Princess Victoria, whilst on holiday with her mother, the Duchess of Kent, at Norris Castle.

St.James's, like Holy Trinity Bembridge, was very plain and disgracefully cheap [1] and quite small. It was very soon outgrown by the Parish and demolished, save for the tower, in which, was the foundation stone laid by Princess Victoria. It was replaced by a much grander building between the years 1864 to 1868. In 1870 a fine chancel was added, a gift from Dowager Viscountess Gort wife of the third Viscount of East Cowes Castle.

1 - Summerson 1980 (C4, P155).

19. BARTON MANOR FARM, EAST COWES. Undated.

Barton Manor Estate, during the early nineteenth century was one of the foremost Island estates.

Adjoining the Georgian estate of Osborne it was also quite close to Nash's country estate. A large rustic farm cottage at the estate farm is credited to Nash [1] which incorporated a drawing room and dining-room with canted bay windows and columned loggias. Barton Manor was acquired by Queen Victoria after 1845 and became part of the Osborne Estate.

The building has long since disappeared.

1 - Mansbridge 1991.

20.   SPRING HILL HOUSE, EAST COWES. Undated,

A two storeyed house with a canted bay window is shown in plan and elevation in George Repton's Brighton sketchbook. The plan also makes several references to the name Goodrich, a family who were believed to be in residence at Spring Hill from 1796.

The ground floor included a dining-room, 'parlour' and storeroom with the kitchen and offices situated in the basement. The first floor accommodation included two large bedrooms for the Goodriches and the servants garrets.

Nash's diary of 1832 mentions a Miss Goodrich, who was a visitor to the castle and joined the Nashes for local walks.

21.   VILLA FOR LORD BELFAST, WEST COWES c1832

Nash's diary of 1832 records on 21 January 'Went to Cowes to see Lord Belfast's new building' and on 14 February 'Sent Lord Belfast his plans.'

Barber [1] refers to Lord Belfast's and Lord Grantham's villas as located on the left side of West Cliff proceeding towards Egypt. West Cliff was the continuation of the parade along the line of the shore.

It would seem therefore that Nash either designed the villa or presented plans for alterations, the details of which do not survive.

1 - Barber 1845

A small concrete road called John Nash Avenue is the principal entrance into the urban development that now covers what was once East Cowes Castle Estate. Elsewhere there is a road called Vereker Drive, acknowledging the generosity of the titled family, that lived in the castle for many years.

There is little else to recount the presence of John Nash. Names of local interest are recorded on the remaining estate roads, the opportunity not taken to introduce names of particular relevance to Nash and his castle-house architecture. Garnstone, Ravensworth, Caerhays and Knepp more apposite perhaps and evoking inquiring thoughts of a man who might be considered the second most famous former resident of East Cowes and who, from 1802 until 1835, was Seigneur of East Cowes Castle.

68. Northwood House, West Cowes c1807 : Nash undertook a number of commissions to remodel and extend Northwood House for the Estate Owner Mr G. Ward.

69. West Cowes 1815 : from a water colour by Tom Pennethorne. The tower of Nash's Northwood Church is a prominent feature in this rare picture.

70. Nunwell House Brading, from an engraving by T.Barber c1834 :Nash's proposals to replace
the sixteenth century house were not adopted but his extensive stable block is now the
main residence.

71. Hamstead, c1835 : Nash's considerable cottage style manor, extensively remodelled during
his lifetime.

72. Isle of Wight Institution, from an engraving by George Brannon 1821 : the building remains much as designed by Nash.

73. St.Mildred's Church Whippingham, from an engraving by E.Roberts 1816 : Nash's picturesque church was replaced by the present Victorian building in 1861.

74. Hillgrove & Trinity Church Bembridge : from an engraving by G.Brannon 1832.

75. Guildhall, Newport : remains substantially as designed by Nash, from an engraving by
    T.Barber 1834.

76. Hippisley House : Nash's Gothic villa adjacent to Cowes Castle, from an engraving by G.Brannon 1825.

77. St.James's Church, East Cowes : the tower and Nash Sarcophagus is all that remains of the original little Gothic church.

Appendix I

JOHN NASH ARCHITECT 1752-1835

BIOGRAPHICAL REFERENCE

1752	-	Born of Welsh parents most certainly in Lambeth
1758/59	-	Orphaned aged 6 on death of father
1766-75	-	Articled to Sir Robert Taylor noted Palladian architect, Westminster
1775	-	Married to Jane Elizabeth Kerr, Newington, London
1777	-	Bloomsbury Square/Great Russel Street Venture
1778-81	-	Living in Great Russel Street
1762	-	Divorce proceedings
1783	-	Declared bankrupt as a Carpenter; Dealer and Chapman
1784	-	Stripped of all property but a free man
1784	-	Living in Wales
1785-9	-	Minor Works in Wales
1787	-	The procurement of the act of divorce
1789-92	-	Important commissions in Wales
1790	-	First Meeting with Humphry Repton
1792	-	Auguste Charles de Pugin joins the office
1793	-	Visited the Isle of Wight for the first time
1794-5	-	Castle House, Aberystwyth (Nash's encounter with the picturesque *avant-garde*)
1795	-	Living both in Wales and London
1795	-	First major commission in England, Kentchurch Court

1778

Early Works

1796

Appendix 1

Year	Event		
1796	–	Partnership with Humphry Repton and his son John Adey joins the office	**1796**
1797	–	Leased No 28 and 29 Dover Street	
1798	–	Married Mary Anne Bradley, Hanover Square, London	
1798	–	Purchased land at East Cowes	
1798	–	First introduced to Prince of Wales	
1799	–	John Adey Repton leaves the office	
1800	–	Partnership with Humphrey Repton dissolved	
1802	–	East Cowes Castle; first stage completed George Stanley Repton joins the office	Country Houses in England & Ireland
1806	–	Purchased Hamstead	
1806	–	Appointed as salaried architect to Office of Woods & Forests	
1812	–	Commenced Regents Park	
1814	–	Appointed with others as architect to Board of Works	
1815	–	Royal Pavilion Brighton	
1817	–	Commenced Regent Street	
1820-21	–	Constructs 14-16 Regent Street	
1825	–	Buckingham Palace	
1827	–	Plans St James Park	
1830	–	Dismissed as architect for Buckingham Palace	
1834	–	Resigned London practice to James Pennethorne	
1835	–	Died at East Cowes Castle 13th May	

Right-hand bracket annotations:

1810 — **1811** — Works for the Prince Regent — **1818** — **1820**

1810 — Works in London for the Office of Woods & Forests and Board of Works — **1830** — **1833**

Appendix II

i WORKS COMPLETED BY NASH

Aberayron, Cards.**c1807**. Replanning and development.

Abergavenny, Mon. Market House **1794-95.** Since demolished

Aberystwyth Bridge, Cards.**c1798**. Replaced in **1886.**

Adult Orphan Asylum, Regents Park **1824**. Since demolished.

Albury, Surrey, date unknown. Bridge for Samuel Thornton, no longer existing. 2

All Souls', Langham Place, London. **1822.**

Aqualate Hall, Staffs. **1808**. For Sir John F.Boughey, Bt. Since demolished.

Aroid House, Kew Gardens. **1836**. Garden Pavillion moved from Buckingham Palace.

Ascot, Royal Stand. **1821**. For George IV, since demolished.

Atcham, Shropshire. **1797.** For Lord Berwick improvements and cottages.

Attingham Hall, Shropshire.**c1805**. For Lord Berwick; alterations and additions. 1

Bagshot House, Bagshot, Surrey. **1818.** Alterations and improvements for the Crown. Demolished after **1861.**

Bank Farm, Kingston-upon-Thames.**c1796.** For Major-General St John, since demolished.

Barnsley Park, Gloucs. **1806-1810.** For J Musgrave. BT. Additions and decorations.

Barr Hall, Great Barr, Staffs.**c1800**. Alterations, part demolished. 1

Belmont Clehonger, Herefordshire. Undated. Estate Lodge for Dr John Matthews.

Betley Court, Staffs. **1807-10.** Alterations for Sir Thomas Fletcher.

Blaise Hamlet Henbury, Gloucestershire. **1810-1811**. Picturesque Cottages.

Blaise Castle House, Henbury, Gloucestershire.**c1796** for J S Harford Conservatory and Cottages. 1

Bloomsbury Square, No 17 and adjoining houses in Great Russell Street. **1778.** Altered, but still existing.

Brampton Park, Brampton, Huntingdownshire. **1806-1810.** For Lady Olivia Sparrow improvements.

Brickyard Lane Cottage, Carmarthen.**c1785**. Demlished **1858.**

Brighton, Royal Pavilion. **1815-23.** For the Prince Regent.

Buckingham Palace. **1825-30.** For George IV.

Bulstrode.**c1800**. For the Duke of Portland; alterations not now existing.

Bushey House, Hampton, Middlesex. **1808**. For Duke of clarence, improvements.

Caerhayes Castle, Cornwall.**c1808**. For J Trevanion.

Cahir Co. Tipperary. undated. Protestant Church.

Caledon House, Co. Tyrone **c1812.** For 2nd Earl of Caledon; alterations and additions.

Caledon Church Spire.**1802**

Cardigan Gaol. **1793**. Demolished.

Carmarthon Church. **1785**. New roof and ceiling. Since demolished.

Carlton House, London. **1813**. For the Prince Regent; alterations and decorations, since demolished.

Carlton House Garden. **1814**. Polygon Room. Removed to Woolwich.

Carlton Mews, St James's. **1827-1829**. For the Crown. Since demolished.

Carmarthen Gaol.**1789-92**. Demolished **1938.**

Casina, Dulwich. **1797.** For Richard Shawe 2

Castle House, Aberystwyth.**c.1793**. For Uvedale Price. Since demolished.

Chalfont House, Bucks.**c1800**. Exterior remodelled for Thomas Hibbert. 1

Charborough Park, Dorset.**c1810.** Alterations for Richard Erle Drax Governor.

Childwall Hall, Lancs.**c1805**. For Bamber Gascoyne, M.P., since demolished.

Clarence House, St James's.**1825**. For the Duke of Clarence; remodelled **1873.**

Clytha Castle, Monmouthshire.**1790.** For William Jones.

Colby Lodge, Tenby. Updated for the Colby Family.

Corsham Court, Wilts.**1797**. For P.C. Methuen, additions and alterations. 1

County Fire Office, London.**1819**. For the Crown; with Robert Abraham, since demolished.

Cowdray Park, Midhurst, Sussex. Undated. Heated conservatory for William Poyntz M.P. 2

Crawfordsburn, Nr Bangor, County Down. Date unknown. Lodge for John Crawford.

Cronkhill, Shropshire.**c1802**. For Lord Berwick.

Cumberland Lodge, Windsor Great Park. **1814**. Repairs for the Crown.

Derryloran, Parish Church, Cookstown, Co.Tyrone.**1822.**

Dolaucothi, Carmarthenshire.**1792-95**. For John Johnes; alterations, now in ruins.

Downton Castle, Herefordshire.(Between **1782-1805)** For Richard Payne Knight. Remodelled octagonal tower.

Dover Street, No 29.**1798.** Nash's own house, since demolished.

Exeter College, Oxford.**1815-18**. Hall repairs. 1

Farningham.**1778.** Mausoleum.

Ffynone, Pembs.**1793.** For Capt. Colby.

Foley House, Haverfordwest, Pembs.**1793.** For Richard Foley.

Garnstone, Herefords.**c1806.** For Samuel Peploe, since demolished.

Gelli-Tal-Sarn, Cards.Undated. Extension block and rustic gatehouse.

Glanwysc, Liangattock, Breconshire.**c1795.** Villa for Admiral Gell, since remodelled.

Golden Grove, Carmarthen.**1787.** Bathroom for John Vaughan, since demolished.

Goodwood, Sussex.**c1807.** Additions for the Fourth Duke of Richmond.

Gracefield Lodge, Co.Kildare.**1817.** For Mrs Kavanagh.

Green Gardens, Carmarthen.**c1785.** Plain two storey house for himself.

Hafod, Cards.**1793.** For Col Thomas Johnes; alterations and additions, since demolished.

Hale Hall, Lancs.**c1806.** For John Blackburne, M.P.; south front, since demolished.

Harmonic Institution, No 246 Regent Street.**1819.** Since demolished.

Harpton Court, Radnorshire.**c1805.** For Frankland Lewis. 2

Haymarket Theatre, London.**1820.**

Helmingham Hall, Suffolk.**1800**. Alterations for the 6th Earl of Dysart.

Hereford Gaol.**1796.** Since demolished.

Highgate Hill Tunnel.**1813.** For Highgate Archway Co.; construction of viaduct, demolished 1901.

High Legh Hall, Cheshire.**c1806.** For George John Legh; interior fittings, cottages, farm buildings, etc. 1

Hollycombe, Sussex.**c1805.** For Charles Taylor, since rebuilt. 2

Hopton Court, Salop.**1811-13.** Additions for Thomas Botfield.

Hothfield Place, Hothfield, Kent.**c1800.** For Lord Thanet, farm buildings and estate cottages. 2

Ingestre Hall, Staffs.**1808-13.** For Lord Talbot; restoration, burnt in **1882**. Since demolished.

Jeremy's Hotel, Carmarthon.**c1786.**

Jesus College, Oxford.**1815-18**. Alterations.

Kensington Palace, London.**1816-1825**. Repairs and improvements for the Crown.

Kentchurch Court, Herefordshire.**c1795.** For John Scudamore; Gothic remodelling.

Kildress Church, Co. Tyrone. Updated ceiling

Killymoon Castle, Co. Tyrone. **c1802.** For Colonel William Stewart, M.P.

Kilwaughter Castle, Co. Antrim.**1807**. For Edward Jones Agnew; now in ruins.

King's Mews, Charing Cross.**1816-1824**. Replanning.

King's Opera House, London.**1820**. For the Crown; rebuilt **1893**.

King's Road, London.**1824**. Laying out.

Kingston House, London. Undated. For Lord Listowel; alterations, since demolished.

Knepp Castle, Sussex.**1809**. For Sir Charles Burrell, Bt. 2

Langham House, Crown Estate.**1813-15.** For Sir James Langham M.P.; since demolished.

Leamington, Warwickshire.**1827**. Layout of estate for E Willes.

Lissan Rectory, Co. Tyrone.**1807**. For the Rev. John Staples.

Llanaeron, Cardingamshire.**c1794.** For Major Lewis

Llanfechan, Llanwnon, Cards.**1786**. House for Admiral Thomas; since demolished.

Llysnewydd, Cardiganshire.**c1795**. For Colonel Lewes. Since demolished.

Longner Hall, Shropshire.**1806**. For Robert Burton. 2

Lough Cutra Castle, Co. Galway.**1815**. For Charles Vereker, M.P.

Luscombe Castle, Devon.**c1800.** For Charles Hoare. 1

Marble Arch, London.**1829**. For George IV.

Merly House, Dorset.**c1805.** For Mr Willett; stables. 2

Moccas Court, Herefordshire.**c1805.** For Sir George Cornewall; lodges and cottages. 2

Monachty, Near Aberayeron.**c1808.** For Rev. Gwynne.

Newman Street.**1820-21**. Picture Gallery for Sons of Bejamin West.

New Park, Lyndhurst, Hants.**c1795.** Cottage. 2

Newport Bridge, Monmouthsire.**1791**. Not completed.

Newton Park, Newton St Loe, Somerset.**1796**. For William Gore-Langton M.P. improvements. 1

Northerwood, Near Lyndhurst, Hants.**1810**. Improved.

Opthalmic Hospital, Albany Street, London.**1818**. Nash's own speculation, since demolished.

Parnham, Dorset.**c1810.** For Sir W. Oglander; Gothic additions.

Picton Monument, Carmarthen.**1825**. Since demolished.

Preshaw House, Hampshire.**1810**. For W.Long; Gothic additions.

Ravensworth Castle, Co. Durham.**1807**. For Sir Thomas Liddell, since demolished.

Regent's Canal, London.**1820** (Opened).

Regents Park, London. From 1812. For the Crown.

Designs for terraces, lodges and other buildings in Regents Park including: Park Crescent **1913** (rebuilt **1963-65**) Sussex Place **1822,** Hanover Terrace **1822**; York Terraces, East and West, and York Gate **1822,** Park Square, Ulster Terrace and St Andrew's Place, **1823-26**; Cambridge Terrace, **1824**; Chester Terrace, **1825**; Cumberland Terrace, **1826**; Kent Terrace, **1826**; Lodges at Hanover Gate and Gloucester Gate; Houses in Park Village East and West.

Regent Street, London. From **1817**. For the Crown.

Designs for elevations in Regent Street including: Waterloo Place **1815**; Oxford Circus, **1815**; Piccadilly Circus, **1818**; The Quadrant, **1819**; all since demolished.

Elevations in Suffolk Street and Suffolk Place, **1820**; Carlton House Terrace and Carlton Gardens, **1827-33**; The Strand, William IV Street and Adelaide Street, including the Lowther Arcade **1830.**

Regent Street, London Nos 14-16.**1820-21**. For himself and John Edwards. Since demolished.

Regent Street, London No 15.**1819**. For C.T. Blicke. Since demolished.

Rheidol Bridge, Aberystwyth, Cards.**1792**. Swept away **1886**. 2

Rheola, Neath.**c1812**. For John Edwards; enlargement of small house. 2

Rockingham, Co.Roscommon.**1810**. For Lord Lorton of Boyle; since burnt down and demolished.

Royal Lodge (The King's Cottage), Windsor.**1813-16**. For George IV; rebuilt. Since demolished.

Royal Mews, Buckingham Palace.**1822-1824.** For George IV.

Royal Opera House, Haymarket **1816-1818.** Since demolished.

St Beadh Church, Ardcarn, Co Roscommon.**c.1810.** Alterations.

St Cross Hospital, Winchester. **1827-29** Restoration.

St David's Cathedral, Pembrokeshire. **1793**. West front; now replaced.

St David's Church, Carmarthen.**1825-1827.** Built to Nash's design, completed after his death.

St James's Palace, London. **1821**. For the Crown; state rooms.

St James's Park, London. **1814**. Bridge and pagoda for festivities of **1814.** Demolished.

St James's Park, London. **1814** and later. For the Crown; laying out.

St James's Square, London.**1817** Aud **1822**. Laying out and landscaping.

St John's Church, Caledon, Co Tyrone.**1808**. Timber spire, replaced **1830.**

St Loran's Church, Cookstown, County Tyrone.**c.1822**. Since altered.

St Martins-In-The-Fields. **1830**. Vicarage, vestry hall and National School.

St Marys, Isle Kirkcudbrignt.**c1796.** For Lord Selkirk; cottage and mausoleum. 2

St Marys, Haggerston, London. **1826**. Destroyed by bombs, **1940**.

St Pauls's Church, Cahir, County Tipperary.**1818** and adjacent School House

St Peter's, Carmarthen.**c1786.** Repairs to roof; collapsed **1860**.

Sandridge Park, Devon. **1805**. For Lady Ashburton. Since demolished.

Sarsden House, Oxfordshire.**1795-1796.** For John Langston, improvements, lodges and a bridge. Not all existing. 1

Shanbally Castle, Co. Tipperary. **1818-19** for the Earl of Lismore, since demolished.

Shane's Castle, Co. Antrim.**c1812.** For Earl O'Neill, since burnt down.

Shirburn Park, Watlington, Oxfordshire.**1803.** Estate buildings and orangery. 2

Sion House, Tenby.**c1790.** For William Routh, since burnt down and demolished.

Six Bells, Carmarthen.**c1786.**

Someries House, Regent's Park, London.**c.1824.** Demolished.

Southborough Place, Surrey. **1808**. For Thomas Langley.

Southgate Grove, London. **1797**. For Walker Gray. 1

Standford Bridge, Worcestershire. **1795**. For Sir Edward Winnington.

Stonelands, Dawlish Devon.**c1817.** For the Hoare family.

Stud House, Hampton Court Palace.**1818** and **1821**. Enlargement and improvements for the Crown.

Suffolk Street, Gallery London. **1823**.

Sundridge Park, Kent. **1799**. For Claude Scott. 1

Temple Druid, Pembrokeshire.**c1795.** For H Bulkeley.

The Market House, Chichester, Sussex.**1807.** Since altered.

The Park, Harrow on the Hill, Middlesex. For Richard Page.**c1895-1803.** Since demolished.

The Priory, Cardigan, Cards.**c1795.** For Col. Thomas Johnes, since altered.

The Strand, 430-449 London.**1830.** Metropolitan improvements; since altered.

The Warrens, Bramshaw near Lyndhurst.**c1805.** For Mr Eyre. 2

Trev-Cefel Bridge Cards. **1793**; since demolished.

United Service Club, London. **1824-28.**

Uppark, Sussex. Undated.**c1800.** For Sir H Fetherstonhaugh; alterations.

Warrens Hotel, No 1 Regent St. **1815**. Since demolished.

Waterloo Place. From **1815**. For the Crown.

West Grinstead Park, Sussex.**c1809.** For Walter Burrell, now in ruins. 2

West Strand improvements, London **1826-1831**

White Lodge, Richmond Park, Surrey.**1814**. For Lord Sidmouth, additions.

Whitson Court, Newport, Mon.**c1795**. For W Phillips.

Witley Court, Worc.**c1805**. For Lord Foley; alterations. 2

Worcester Park, near Ewell, Surrey. Before **1826**. Enlarged.

Dates refer to commencement of building or period of construction. This list is not exhaustive and does not include projects often exhibited at the Royal Academy during Nash's life - numerous cottages, stables and other small buildings for Royal Parks and Forests and for Repton's and Nash's clients.

The listed works include early works from **1778-97** Country houses in England and Ireland from **1796-1818**, works for the Prince Regent from **1811-20**, works in London for the Office of Woods, Forests and Land Revenues from **1810-14,** The London Works independently commissioned, Royal Buildings **1820-30**, works for the Commissioners for building new churches and miscellaneous works. It does not include works undertaken on the Isle of Wight as these are detailed in Chapter 5.

ii WORKS ATTRIBUTED TO NASH

Antony House, Torpoint, Cornwall.**1803**. Gate Lodge for Reginald Pole - Carew 1 2

Chapel Street, Nos 80-82, Cookstown, Co.Tyrone. Undated, Dowager House for Mr Stewart.

Fenaghy House, Ballymena, Co. Antrim. Undated. Gate Lodge.

Glaslough Castle, Co. Monaghan. Undated. Gatehouse.

Hawarden Castle, Flintshire.**1807**. Nash's design for Castellation,, implemented by others.

Hilton Park, Near Essington, Staffordshire.**1796**. For Henry Vernon. Estate cottage; not now existing.

Holwood House, Keston, Kent.**1799**. Estate cottage for William Pitt M.P. Not now existing. 1

Houghton Lodge, Houghton, Hants.**c1800.**

Hyde Park, London.**1804** and **1824**. Cottage and gardens; not now existing. 2

The Swiss Cottage, Cahir Park, Co. Tipperary.**1810-1814**. Restored.

Tynan Abbey, Co.Armagh.**c1816.** Alterations for Sir James Stronge.

Whitehall, Winestead, Yorks. **1814-1815**. For Arthur Maister.

Woodhall, Ellerby, Yorks.**1814-1815**. For Henry William Maister.

Woodpark Lodge, Killylea, Co.Armargh. Undated, in ruins.

1   *Completed in association with Humphry Repton.*
2   *Illustrated within George Repton's R.I.B.A Sketch Books.*

Appendix III

EAST COWES CASTLE AND ESTATE
INTERESTING STATISTICS

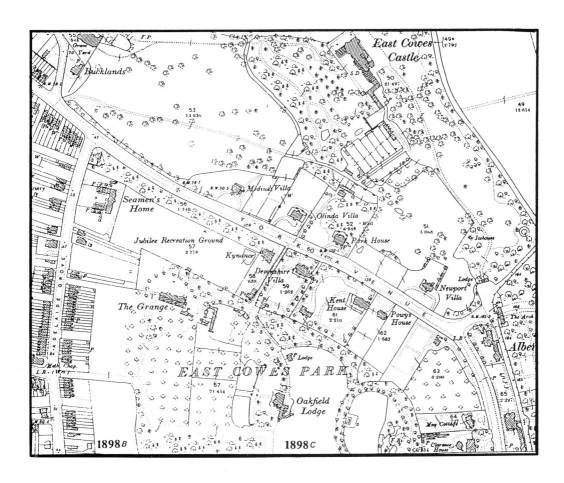

Estate area - approximately 50 acres (20.23 Hectares) as purchased by Nash 1798 and 1800

Extreme length of building - 350 feet (106.68 metres)

Extreme width of building - 130 feet (39.63 metres)

Drive length - North Lodge to Castle entrance - 230 yards (210.3 metres)

Drive length - South Gate to Castle Entrance - 450 yards (411.3 metres)

Kitchen garden dimensions - 150 feet x 200 feet approximately (45.72 x 60.96 metres)

Appendix IV

GLOSSARY OF ARCHITECTURAL TERMS
USED IN THE TEXT

Antefixa	-	An upright ornament at the eaves of a tiled roof to hide joints or at the edge of a ridge or frieze
Anthemion	-	Leaf design used in architecture
Ashlar	-	Squared stone masonry
Baluster	-	Post supporting handrail of a staircase
Bartizan	-	A turret with loopholes jutting out from a wall
Battlement	-	A parapet mounted alternatively with raised portions
Bay Window	-	Projecting window with square or canted sides from a wall face
Capital	-	The top section of a column or pilaster
Castellated	-	Dressed with battlements
Cavetto	-	A moulding having concave profile of not more than 90° curvature terminating in a vertical fillet with a projection usually about equal to its altitude.
Colonnade	-	A row of columns linked at their heads by a horizontal beam, entablature or series of arches.
Colonette	-	A small column
Corbels	-	A projection from a wall to act as a support for a superimposed member
Cornthiam	-	Classical style of column governed by its own proportions
Cornice	-	The projecting band at the top of a wall or the top section of entablature
Cottage Orné	-	An ornamental cottage typical of the picturesque movement, built on an estate or park for effect, the aesthetics being more important than the practicality.
Coursed Rubble	-	Masonry composed of irregular or broken stone
Crenellation	-	Having battlements or loopholes
Curtain Wall	-	The lengths of wall built between the towers of a castle or a wall surrounding a castle or part there of.
Doric	-	Classical style of column governed by its own proportions.

Embrasure	-	The bevelling of the inside of the wall openings for a window or door, the indents or crenelles of a battlement.
Entablature	-	In classical architecture the horizontal structure above the columns subdivided into three sections in descending order cornice, freeze and architrave.
Ionic	-	Classical style of inset columns.
In-Antis	-	The alignment of inset columns.
Label	-	A square decorative moulding over a window to divert rain water.
Loggia	-	An open gallery, usually behind a colonnade
Machicolation	-	In castellated architecture, a parapet projecting in advance of a wall face with openings for defensive purposes.
Ogee	-	A S shaped curve
Oriel Window	-	A bay window built out from a wall above ground level.
Pediment	-	The crowning part of a portico usually triangular, sometimes segmented and contained within the divided cornice.
Pendant	-	A hanging ornament
Pier	-	Solid masonry support, with the same function as a column
Pilaster	-	A shallow usually square pier projecting from a wall
Pinnacled	-	Slender turret elevated above main roof level
Porte-cochère	-	A covered porch of such proportions to allow access for wheeled vehicles
Portico	-	Centre piece of a house or church with classical columns and a pediment, it may be one or more stories high.
Rusticated	-	Masonry laid with deep wide joints used to give texture and the impression of strength.
Screen Wall	-	A non-structural partition wall used to divide space.
Spandrell	-	Space between the outer curves of an arch and the head section
Stucco	-	A fine plaster for walls or their relief ornaments usually composed of Portland cement, sand and a small amount of lime.
Tracery	-	The intersection in various ways of the mullions of a window, a Gothic architectural feature.
Tympana	-	The triangular or semi circular face of a pediment between the horizonal and the raking cornices.
Ovolo	-	Convex moulding or quarter round

East Cowes Castle

Appendix V

FURTHER READING

Barber, T.	-	*Barbers Picturesque Illustrations of The Isle of Wight 1845*, (reprinted 1973)
Davis, T.	-	*The Architecture of John Nash* **1960**
Davis, T.	-	*John Nash, The Prince Regent's Architect* **1966**
Mansbridge, M.	-	*John Nash, A Complete Catalogue* **1991**
Peacocke, M.	-	*Buckingham Palace* **1951**
Saunders, A.	-	*A 'Regents Park'* **1969**
Summerson, J.	-	*John Nash, Architect to King George IV* **1935**
Summerson, Sir J.	-	*The Life and Work of John Nash, Architect* **1980**
Various Authors	-	*Buckingham Palace, A Complete Guide* **1993**

Foot Note:-

Before his death in 1992, Sir John Summerson arranged to have the diaries of John Nash transcribed for publication, accompanied by his notes and introduction, as a fitting conclusion to this work on Nash over the years.

This pictorial contains a number of these diary entries and therefore appropriately heralds the forthcoming publication of Sir John's final work.

Index

Aberayron, 76
Abergavenny, 76
Aberystwyth, 14, 22, 76
Adult Orphan Asylum, 76
Albany Street, 44
Albert Grove, 52
Albert, Prince, 52, 70
Adelaide Street, 80
Agenew, Edward Jones, 79
All Souls Langham Place, 76
Anthony House, 82
Aqualate Hall, 76
Arnold, Lady Mary, 46
Aroid House, 76
Ascot, 76
Ashburton, Lady, 81
Atcham, 76
Atkinson, Mr., 42
Attringham Park, 76

Bagshot House, 76
Bank Farm, 76
Barber, T., 49,67,73,86
Barnsley Park, 76
Barr Hill, 76
Barton, Miss, 40
Barton Manor Farm, 63,72,73
Baugh, Rev., 46
Becford, Capt., 42
Belfast, Lord, 40,41,63,73
Bellevue Estate, 20,65
Belmont Clohanger, 76
Bernasconi, 46
Berwick, Lord, 76, 77
Betley Court, 76
Bettsworth, John, 59
Blatchford, 22,41
Blackburne, John M.P., 78
Blaise Castle House, 76
Blaise Hamlet 26,76
Blicke, C.T.,80
Bloomfield, Mrs., 41
Bloomsbury, 14,74,76
Blore, Edward, 37,42
Botfield Thomas, 78
Boyle, Lord, 41
Brampton Park, 76
Brannon, G., 12,29,67,72
Brickyard Lane Cottage, 76
Brighton, 16,39

British Museum, 12
Brown, 'Capability', 16
Browne, 38,39
Buckingham House (Palace),13,24,31,33,37,39,44,48,
75,76,80,(Fig.8)
Bulkeley, H., 81
Bulstrode, 76
Burrell, Sir Charles, 60,79
Burrell, Walter, 60,82
Burton, Decimus, 48
Burton, Robert, 79
Burwell N., 50
Bushey House, 77

Caerhays Castle, 56,59,77
Cahir Church, 77
Caledon Church, 77
Caledon, Earl of, 77
Caledon House, 77
Cambridge Terrace, 80
Campbell, Col., 41
Campbell, Mrs., 42
Cardigan Goal, 77
Cardigan Priory, 81
Carlton House, 31,33,37
Carlton House Gardens, 34,65,77,80
Carlton House Stables, 40
Carlton Mews, 77
Carlton Terrace, 34,44,46
Carltons, The, 41,42
Carmarthen Goal, 77
Casina, 77
Castle House, 14,15,22,55,74,77 (Fig.2)
Chalfont House, 77
Chamberlaine, W.,22
Chapel Street, 82
Chapman, Miss, 39
Charborough Park, 77
Charing Cross, 39,79
Charles I, 68
Chester Terrace, 80
Chichester Market House, 81
Childwall Hall, 56,58,77
Clarence, Duke of (William IV), 77
Clarence House, 77
Clytha Castle, 77
Cockerell, C.R., 29
Cockerell, S.P., 29
Colby, Capt., 77,78
Colby Lodge, 77

Copley, Mrs., 42
Cornewall, George, 79
Corsham Court, 16,77
County Fire Office, 77
Covent Garden, 48
Cowdray Park, 77
Coxe-Hippisley, Sir J, 63,72
Crawford, John, 77
Crawfordsburn, 77
Cronk Hill, 77
Cubitt, Thomas, 52
Cumberland Lodge, 77
Cumberland Terrace, 80

David, Mr., 42
Davis, Terrance, 7,12,18,86
Debourne Estate, 20,65
Delafield, Mr., 40
Derryloran Church, 77
Dolaucothie, 77
Dover Street, 18,28,75,77 (Fig.3)
Downton, Downton Castle, 14,15,22,55,77
Ducannon, Lord, 40
Dulcie, Earl of, 71
Dulwich, 77
Duncan, Mr., 41
Dysart, Earl of, 78

East Cowes Castle;
        Site 20,
        Building 22,
        Sale 49,
        Demolition 53
East Shamblers 22,50,80
Eastwick, 39, 41
Edwards, John, 28,29,35,44
Elm Cottage, 63,67
Erle-Drax, Richard, 77
Evans, Booksellers, 49
Evans, Richard, 49
Exeter College, 78
Eyre, Mrs., 81

Farington, Joseph, 12,24,26,29,30,38,55
Farnborough, Lord, 31
Farningham Masoleum, 78
Featherstonhaugh, Sir Harry, 81
Fenaghy House, 82
Ffyhone, 78
Fletcher, Sir Thomas, 76
Fochier-de-Lambert, 20
Foley, Capt. R., 78
Foley House, 78
Foley, Lord, 82
Fountain Inn, 63,72

Garnstone Castle, 56,58,73,78
Gelli-Tal-Sarn, 78

Gascoyne, Bamber, M.P., 58,77
Gatcombe, 41
Gell, Admiral, 78
George III, 31
Glanwysc, 78
Glaslough Castle, 82
Gloucester Gate, 80
Golden Grove, 78
Goodrich, Mr., 40,41,73
Goodwood, 78
Gore-Loughton, William, M.P., 79
Golding, Sir W., 42
Gort, Dowager, Viscountess, 72
Gort (Vereker) Family, 52,73
Gort, Viscount, 50,61,72
Gouldbourne, 33
Gracefield Lodge, 78
Gray, Lord, 40
Gray, Robert, 28
Gray, Walker, 81
Great Russel Street, 74,76
Green Gardens, 78
Grey, Lord, 41
Guy, Arthur, 53
Gwynne, Rev. A.T., 79

Hafod, 14,78
Hale Hall, 78
Hamstead, 22,30,42,45,49,63,68,70,75, (Fig.13)
Hanover Gate, 80
Hanover Terrace, 80
Harford, J.S., 76
Hargreaves, A., 61
Harmonic Institution, 78
Harpton Court, 65,68,70,78
Harwarden Castle, 82
Haymarket, 78
Heathfield, 41,63,68,70
Helmingham Hall, 78
Hereford Goal, 78
Hewitt, Col.William, 39
Hewitt, Mr.& Mrs., 39,40,46
Hibbert, Thomas, 77
Highgate Archway, 78
Highgate Hill Tunnel, 78
High Leigh, 78
Hill, Archdeacon, 46
Hillgrove, 63,71,72
Hilton Park, 82
Hippisley House, 63,72
Hippisley, Sir John Coxe, 72
Hoare, Charles, 57,79,81
Hoffins, Mr., 42
Hopkinson, 41
Hollycombe, 78
Holmes, Sir Leonard, 70,71
Holmes, Lady, 41
Holwood House, 82

Index

Holy Trinity Church, 63,72
Hook, Theodore, 47,71
Hook, Walter, 41,71
Hopton Court, 78
Hothfield Place, 78
Houghton Lodge, 82
Hyde Park, 82

Ingestre Hall, 78
Isle of Wight, 14,18,63,74
Isle of Wight, Institution, 63,70
Isle of Wight Guildhall, 63,71

James, Mrs., 42
Jeremey's Hotel, 78
Jesus College, 78
Johnes, John, 77
Johnes, Col. Thomas, 78
Johnes, Thomas, 81
Johnes, William, 14,78
Jones, Agnew-Edward, 59,79
Jones, William, 77

Kavanagh, Mrs., 78
Kensington Palace, 78
Kent, Duchess of, 39,72
Kent Terrace, 80
Kentchurch Court, 74,78
Kerr, Jane, Elizabeth, 74
Kildress Church, 78
Killymoon Castle, 42,56,58,79
Killwaughter Castle, 56,59,79
King's Mews, 79
King's Opera House, 79
King's Road, 79
Kingston House, 79
Knepp Castle, 56,60,79
Knight, Richard Payne, 14,16,77
Knighton, William, 38

Lambert, Mr., 67
Lambeth, 74
Langham House, 79
Langham, Sir James, 79
Langley, Thomas, 81
Langston, John, 81
Lathorne, Mr., 42
Lawrence, Sir Thomas, 38
Lee, Charles, 65
Leight, G.J., 78
Leamington, 79
Lewes, Col., 79
Lewis, Frankland, 78
Lewis, Major, 79
Liddel, Sir Thomas, 59,80
Lingham, Sir James, 79
Lismore, Earl of, 61,81
Lissan Rectory, 79

Lister, 42
Listowel, Lord, 79
Litloff, Henry, 42
Llanairon, 79
Llanfechan, 79
Llysnewydd, 79
Longner Hall, 79
Lorton, Lord, 80
Lough Cutra Castle, 50,56,61,79
Lowther Arcade, 80
Luscombe Castle, 22,26,56,57,79
Lyon, Mr. & Mrs., 41,42,46

McBride, Admiral, 20
Mainwaring, General, 46
Maister, Arthur, 82
Maister, Henry William, 82
Marlborough Street, 40
Mall The, 34
Mansbridge, M., 7,12,16,63,65,67,68,71,72,73,86
Marble Arch, The., 33,79
Mattews, Dr.J., 76
Melville, Lady, 29
Meryl House, 79
Methuen, P.C., 16,77
Milne, Alexander, 44
Moccas Court, 79
Monarchty, 79
Mount Sylvan, 22
Musgrave, J., BT., 76

Napoleon Bonaparte, 20
Nash, John; (Fig.1),
        Work in Wales, 14,
        Return to London, 18,
        Partnership with Repton 16,
        Quarrel with Repton, 16,
        Marriage 18,
        Work at Buckingham
        House, 31, Retirement, 44
        Illness, 38 and death, 47
Nash, Mrs. John(Mary Anne Bradley),18,28,29,30,45,
46,47,49,70,75
National Gallery, 40,45
New Street, 44
Newman Street, 79
New Park, 79
Newport Bridge, 79
Newport, Isle of Wight, 22, 40,45,68
Newton Park, 79
Ningwood, 22
Nixon, 39,41,46,50
Norris Castle, 20,21,22,29,40,49,72
North Lodge,,26,54
Northerwood, 79
Northwood Church (St Marys), 63,65,67
Northwood House & Park 63,65,67, (Fig.12)
Nunwell House, 63,68

Oglander, Sir William, 46,68,79
O'Neil, Earl, 81
Opthalmic Hospital, 79
Opthalmia, 44,46
Orchard Cottage, 63,67
Osborne Estate (House), 20,22,52,67,70,73
Osborne Cottage, 65,67
Oxford Circus, 80

Page, Richard, 81
Padmore, 42
Pall Mall, 31
Park Crescent, 80
Park Villages, 44,80
Parker, Mrs., 40
Parker, Sophie, 45
Parnham, 68,79
Peacocke, M., 86
Pennethorne, Ann, 29,30,70
Pennethorne, Sir James, 29,30,36,38,39
Pennethorne, John, 29,30,68
Pennethorne, Rose, 68
Pennethorne, Sarah, 29,30,68
Pennethorne, Thomas, 29,30
Peploe, Samuel, 58,78
Phillip, Mr., 45
Phillips, W., 82
Piccadilly Circus, 80
Picton Monument, 79
Picturesque, The, 14,16,20
Pike, W., 70
Pitt, William, M.P., 82
Pole-Carew, Reginald, 82
Portland, Duke of, 76
Poyntz, William, M.P., 77
Preshaw House, 79
Price Uvedale, 14,77
Prince Regent The,(George IV), 26,28,29,30,31,
37,38,41,55,76,77,79,80
Pugin, A.C. de, 30,48,80

Quadrant, The, 45,48,80

Ravensworth Castle, 56,59,73,80
Ravensworth, Lord, 59
R.C.H.M.E., 26,53
Red Books, The 16
Regent's Canal, The, 45,80
Regent's Park, 13,24,34,40,44,48,55,75,80,81
Regent Street, 28,30,39,44,45,49,55,75, (Fig.7)
Repton, J.A., 16,75
Repton, Humphrey, 16,26,53,57,65,74,75,82
Repton, G.S., 16,58,65,67,68,70,71,73,75,82
Rheidol Bridge, 80
Rheola, 80
Richmond, Duke of, 78

Rochester, Bishop of, 42
Rockingham, 80
Routh, William, 81
Royal George, 28,29
Royal Lodge, 80
Royal Mewis, 80
Royal Opera House, 80
Royal Pavillion, The, 24,31,39,75,76

St.Andrew's Place, 80
St.Beadh Church, 80
St.Cross Hospital, 80
St.David's Cathedral, 80
St.David's Church, 80
St.Helens, Lord, 33
St.James's Church, 40,46,63,72
St.James's Palace, 31,80
St.James's Park, 34,40,44,48,75,80
St.James's Square, 80
St.John, Major Gen.,76
St.John's Church, 80
St.John's Ryde, 63,65
St.Loran's Church, 80
St.Martins in the Fields, 48,80
St.Marys, Haggerston, 81
St.Mary's Isle Kirkcudbright, 81
St.Mildred's Church, Whippingham, 63,70
St.Mildred's Rectory, 63,72
St.Paul's Church, 81
St.Peter's Carmarthen, 81
Sandridge Park, 81
Sarsden House, 81
Saunders, A., 86
Saunders, Mr., 42
Sawyer, C., 50
Scott, Claude, 81
Scudamore, John, 78
Selkerk, Lord, 81
Sewell, Mr., 45
Seymour, Lord George, 40,41,42,45,49
Seymour, Lord Henry, 20,29
Sezincote, 29
Shalfleet, 30,40,42
Shanbally Castle, 56,61,62,81
Shanes Castle, 81
Shannon Castle, 49
Shannon, Lord, 49,53
Shawe, Richard, 77
Sheddon, Mr., 45
Shirburn Park, 81
Sidmouth, Lord, 82
Simeon, Edward, 65
Simeon, Sir Richard, 42
Sion House, 81
Six Bells, 81
Slatwoods, 22

Index

Smirke, Sir R., 32
Smith, Mr., 42,45
Soane, Sir John, 31,32
Someries House, 81
Southborough Place, 81
Southampton, 20,22,28,40,44
Southgate Grove, 81
Southgate Lodge, 52,53
Sparrow, Lady Olivia, 76
Stanford Bridge, 81
Spring Hill House, 63,73,
Staples, Rev.John, 79
Stewart, Col.William, 58,78
Stewart, John, 58
Stewart, Mr., 41,58,82
Stonelands, 81
Stronge, Sir James, 82
Strand, The, 80
Stud House, 81
Suffolk Place, 80
Suffolk Street, 34,80,81
Summerson, Sir John, 7,12,26,30,45,67,72,86
Sundridge Park, 81
Sussex Place, 80

Talbot, Lord, 78
Taylor, Charles, 78
Taylor, Sir Robert, 16,74
Temple Druid, 81
Thanet, Lord, 78
The Park, 81
The Swiss Cottage, 82
The Warrens, 81
Thomas, Admiral, 79
Thomas, Sir George, 41
Thompson, Sir Henry, 46
Thornton, Samuel, 76
Tierney, Miss., 41
Trafalgar Square, 33
Trevanion, J., 77
Trev-Cafel Bridge, 81
Turner, J.M.W., 29,30,42,44,49
Tudor, George, 50
Tudor, Mrs, 50
Tynan Abbey, 82

Ulster Terrace, 80
United Services Club, 81
Uppark, 81

Vaughan, John, 78
Vaughan, Mrs., 40,41
Vereker, Charles (Lord Gort), 50,79
Vernon Henry, 82
Victoria, Princess (Queen), 39,52,67,70,71,72,73
Villiers, Miss, 40,42
Vine, Mrs., 42

Wales, Prince of, 18,75
Ward, Charlotte, 39,40,46
Ward, Emma, 39,40,46
Ward, George, 20,29,45,65,67
Ward, G.H., 44,45
Ward, J.R., 46
Ward, Nora, 46
Ward family, 67
Warrens Hotel, 81
Waterloo Place, 48,80,82
Wellington, Duke of, 18,32,35,38,41
West, Benjamin, 30,79
West Cowes, 40,42,44 (Fig.4)
West Grinstead Park, 56,60,82
Westall, William, 44
Westover, 63,70,71
West Strand, 82
Wheeler, 42
Whippingham 20,46,68,70
Whippingham Church 39,41,42,70
White Lodge, 82
White Hall, 82
White, Mr., 42
Whitley Court, 82
Whitson Court, 82
Wilkins, 39
Willies, E., 79
Willett, Mr., 79
William IV, 39
William IV Street, 80
Windsor, 31,33,77
Winnington, Sir Edward, 81
Woodpark Lodge, 82
Worcester Park, 82
Wyatt, James, 16,20
Wyatt, Sir James (Wyatville) 31,32,50

Yarborough, Lord, 46
York Gate, 80
York Terraces, 80